PRAISE FOR *I KNEW YOU'D BE LOVELY*

"Sly and emotionally complex . . . [Black's] unflinching candor allows her to mine extraordinary revelations."

—*Boston Globe*

"Alethea Black's characters are witty [. . .] without turning caustic, and remain mostly cheerful about their uncertain futures—just the kind of people with whom we want to connect."

—Oprah.com

"This debut reads like a dream, with nary a false note . . . a well-balanced collection filled with low-key charm and notable talent."

—*Kirkus Reviews*

"A sense of vulnerable restlessness is betrayed by the otherwise pragmatic characters of Black's strong debut collection."

—*Publishers Weekly*

"An impressive offering, from a strong new voice, of stories about life's desperation."

—Joseph Arellano, *New York Journal of Books*

"Alethea Black is downright brilliant at capturing the restless striving for a self that we all are feeling in this parlous and unsettling age. *I Knew You'd Be Lovely* is a splendidly resonant debut by an important young writer."

—Robert Olen Butler, Pulitzer Prize–winning author of *A Good Scent from a Strange Mountain*

"I heard a smart person say once that short stories were the ideal form to receive and integrate information. Whether it's completely true or not, the idea has stayed with me, and if you were trying to argue the point, *I Knew You'd Be Lovely*, could be held up as exhibit A. Emotionally, no work(s) of fiction ever moved me more thoroughly."

—Leslie Odom Jr., author of *Failing Up*

"With humor, honesty, and wary hope, Alethea Black's stories capture the pain and power of loving fully—and celebrate life's small astonishments amid our shared human search for the divine. *I Knew You'd Be Lovely* is thoughtful, entertaining and, ultimately, powerful."

—Daphne Kalotay, author of *Russian Winter*

"When I came to the end I wanted to read the next page—or write it, but then I realized that there was no more to be said; as in the Navajo prayer, 'In beauty it is finished.'"

—N. Scott Momaday, Pulitzer Prize–winning author of *House Made of Dawn*

"Alethea Black writes with a deceptively light touch, yet her work packs a serious punch . . . There's a spiritual hunger in her stories reminiscent of Flannery O'Connor, combined with a voice that is all her own."

—Sharon Pomerantz, author of *Rich Boy*

"Reading Alethea Black's seemingly effortless prose is like slipping into water—the eerily clear kind, that shows you more than you may want to see."

—Glen Hirshberg, winner of the 2008 Shirley Jackson Award

You've Been So Lucky Already

A MEMOIR

You've Been So Lucky Already

A MEMOIR

ALETHEA BLACK

Little
a

Published by Little A, New York

www.apub.com

Amazon, the Amazon logo, and Little A are trademarks of Amazon.com, Inc., or its affiliates.

ISBN-13: 9781503900592 (hardcover)
ISBN-10: 1503900592 (hardcover)
ISBN-13: 9781503900608 (paperback)
ISBN-10: 1503900606 (paperback)

Cover design by Kimberly Glyder
Interior illustrations by Ilana Blady

Printed in the United States of America
First edition

For the sick and the suffering

What I thought was an end turned out to be a middle.
What I thought was a brick wall turned out to be a tunnel.
What I thought was an injustice
turned out to be a color of the sky.

—Tony Hoagland

CONTENTS

PART I

UNCONCEALMENT

Sometimes you feel that you're already dead and everything that happens has happened already. That's why certain moments seem oddly familiar. You'll be at the dry cleaner, paying for a dress, and when you get back to your car, you'll discover that, in four minutes flat, your miniature dachshund has not only figured out how to open the pizza box with her teeth but has also eaten all the cheese off your pizza. When you catch her, she's still standing there with her paws in the tomato sauce, where the cheese used to be. At first you'll be furious—you were really looking forward to eating that, and you can't believe you were stupid enough to leave a dog alone in a car with cheese—but even as you fume, you'll have this weird kind of déjà vu. *Oh, right. This is the pizza-dog day.* And you'll remember that later on, she's going to have multiple episodes of dairy intolerance all over the rug.

In some ways it's a comforting thought. All your frustrations, all your joys, all the moments when everything went wrong, when it was hard to believe anything would ever feel normal again, when you actually split off from yourself and observed from a slight distance, which seemed safer, especially when your life exploded right at its midpoint, affording you a crystal-clear view of the heartbreak you caused, the love you absorbed, the deaths that unmoored you, the illness that razed your existence to a pile of terrifyingly beautiful rubble—it's comforting to feel that, somehow, you've borne them all before. And you have this shadowy memory that it was worth it, so you'll do it again. You'll do it all again and again.

Because time is a lie. We're just not moving fast enough to see it.

THE UNMASKED SECRETS OF THE UNIVERSE

As a teenager, my closest friend is my father. He calls me "Kiddo" instead of Alethea, and I call him "Daddo" instead of Fischer. He and my mother are in the process of getting divorced, and my mother and I do not get along. I'm the oldest of four girls, but we're all independent. When I'm with my classmates, I only pretend to be interested in Freddy Krueger movies or scouring the mall for the perfect pair of Guess jeans. In truth, I'm happiest by myself. My father enjoys time by himself, too—mostly to tinker on his math formulas in the basement of our house, where I sometimes watch *Creature Double Feature* on an old Sanyo. But even when we're both alone, we're stitched together in our aloneness.

We live a short drive from Cambridge, where my father is a professor at MIT. On Saturdays, he lets us oldest girls come to work with him, and my sister and I steal pillow mints from the receptionist's dish and ride the elevators for fun. He lets us drink espresso. He lets us eat Big Macs for dinner and stay up late to watch *The Love Boat* and *Fantasy Island*. When my youngest sister becomes obsessed with the movie *Dirty Dancing*, he buys the soundtrack and tries to stay relevant by learning the words to all the songs. He sees life as an infinite set of possibilities, and he's not a person who ever uses the words "right" and "wrong." There is no right or wrong in the world of math. There are only numbers.

Although he's a PhD, he hates being called "doctor"; he doesn't even like "mister." He's not interested in the trappings of status, and he's especially leery of fancy language. "Make me a promise," he says one Saturday morning as he lifts his head from a towering stack of papers. "Never say with twenty words what you can say with two."

It's October when I first start noticing things, mysterious things, disturbing things I can't explain. I like October—the slanted light, the soft taps of dry leaves skittering against the sidewalk—so I've been spending a lot of time outdoors. But, at some point, it begins to feel as though someone is following me. More and more often, I stop abruptly and spin around. At night, right before I surrender to sleep, I swear I can hear a voice whispering in a register just beyond my auditory reach. Several times a week, I have unnervingly vivid dreams of Andrew Cook, a classmate who recently died. All these things conspire to make me suspicious about the nature of existence. My father maintains that life on earth is a straightforward, what-you-see-is-what-you-get type deal. But I know there are things he's not telling me.

Alone in my room, I read books by Carl Jung, William James, Arthur Koestler. They have titles like *The Varieties of Religious Experience* and *The Roots of Coincidence*. In one, Jung describes hearing alarmingly loud noises in his empty house one evening and then discovering his mother's bread knife, the steel blade inexplicably broken into pieces.

In another, there's a photograph of the grandfather clock at the George Hotel, in England, that stopped working the exact minute the hotel's proprietor died. I read about Max Planck's experiment in which photons behaved intelligently—choosing the quickest route, rather than the shortest.

Human beings have auras that actually show up in photographs? Dogs seem to know when their owners are coming home? I study a table showing the results of a poll in which 70 percent of the respondents claim to have seen, heard, or been touched by an animal or person they knew was not there. At any given moment, no matter what else I'm doing, an unspoken question beats through my mind. *What is this life?*

Meanwhile, there is strife. We're all waiting for dinner one night, my sister Melissa and I kicking each other under the table while Ashley surreptitiously carves her initials in the thick perimeter wax (something I have taught her to do) and Paige wails for an unknown reason that no one attends. My mother decided at the last minute that she didn't heat up enough ragù, so she's moving back and forth from the dining room to the stove, serving us and stirring the sauce and trying to control the general mayhem, but not exactly succeeding. My father is more immune to our antics, his mind turning inward as he calmly twirls up strands of pasta. When my mother asks if he'd like a second helping of spaghetti—even though she herself has not yet sat down to her first helping—and my father says, "Yes, I would, thank you very much," she dumps the pot of steaming pasta onto his napkined lap.

Later, when we visit North Hampton for a family trip, and I wear my new yellow bikini and matching yellow swim cap that make me feel as though I am an actual ray of living sunshine, she snaps his glasses in half and throws both halves in the ocean. The strife is frightening and nonsensical—*why break the glasses and also toss them away, when clearly one or the other would do?*—but I don't say anything to my father, who stands there blinking. He resembles a mole without his glasses.

He drives a Buick LeSabre station wagon—mammoth and white as a whale—and when he ferries us to school in the morning, down the long slope of Route 2, he plays the soundtrack to *Grease* on an eight-track stereo, while Melissa, Ashley, and I sing along. Sometimes, for a brief moment, my father will sing along, too.

His singing is always ridiculous. But beneath the words, I catch a subtle message: *I know everything is painful right now, and you probably think it's going to go on like this forever, but there are things you don't understand, things that haven't happened yet that are going to change you the way a struck match changes the air.*

One night, well past my bedtime, I hear a soft knock on my door.

"May I come in?"

When I say yes, my pajamaed father pads into the room, wearing his glasses. At six foot five, he's taller than anyone I know, but even while he's still alive, inside a body, he moves softly, like a ghost. I've been doing somersaults in bed, trying to make sparks with my flannel nightgown, but when my father comes in, I stop. His expression is serious. I have no idea what he might feel like discussing at this hour of the night. Once, he knocked on my door just to try to explain how everything in existence could be expressed as a series of ones and zeros. That was a real snooze.

But tonight, he's quiet. He stands beside my bureau long enough that I start to think I'm in trouble. I sometimes go through his desk drawers in the basement, and I recently stole one of his favorite mechanical pencils. When he picks up the Arthur Koestler book, *The Roots of Coincidence*, and calmly studies its black and psychedelic cover, I seize the moment.

"Have you ever had any experiences you couldn't explain?" I ask. For a long moment, my father says nothing. He's one of those people who's completely comfortable with silence; I've witnessed students in a packed auditorium ask him a question, then have to wait two full minutes for a response.

"What type of experience?"

"I don't know. Something that defied logic. Anything that'd suggest there are things going on that we can't see."

"There's plenty going on we can't see!" he says, suddenly more alive. "Wavelengths of light we don't register, particles too small for our eyes. Just as there are sounds we can't hear—there are radio waves coursing through this room right now. But that's just it: they're beyond human perception, so there'd be no way for me to *experience* them."

I can feel my eyes narrowing. Sometimes my father intentionally says things just to annoy me, and this is clearly one of those times. When he's helping me with my math homework and he finds a way to squirrel out of giving me a straight answer, I thwack him on the knuckles with the eraser end of my pencil. But tonight he's beyond my reach.

He sets the book aside, his brow creased. Something bad is coming. I can feel it.

"Why do you pretend there isn't any magic in the world, when it's so obvious there is?" I ask.

His glasses reflect the lamplight; I can't see his eyes. "I never said there wasn't any magic in the world. There's all kinds of magic. Just look at infinity. The set $\{1, 3, 5, 7, 9 \ldots\}$ is actually no smaller than the set $\{1, 2, 3, 4, 5 \ldots\}$." He snaps his fingers. "Magic!"

But his smile is fake. If I could see them, his eyes would give him away. He hasn't come here tonight to discuss the nature of infinity. He's here to tell me that next week, he'll be moving to a room he's rented in another house owned by another family in another town. From now on, I'll see him only on weekends—this is one of the last times he'll ever stand in my doorway. But I don't know that yet. All I know is the prickly static hidden in my nightgown, and the inscrutable brilliance of his lenses, and the sense that my father has something important to tell me, but it's not the important something I've been waiting to hear.

"That's not *magic*," I say, scornfully. "That's just *math*."

CONVERSATIONS WITH ANGELS

In British lit class, I'm assigned to write a paper on the poetry of William Blake. But I don't want to write about Blake's poetry. I'd much rather write about his habit of conversing with angels, especially the archangel Gabriel, who supposedly told Blake he thought Michelangelo had painted a much better angelic portrait than Raphael. The idea of that conversation and Blake's intimate knowledge of angels makes my brain bristle, but I'm too shy to ask my teacher for an alternate assignment. Instead, I feel paralyzed and resentful, and simply don't write anything, asking to stay home from school on the day the assignment is due. The following week, I skip biology and buy a bag of chocolate chip cookies from Purity Supreme to eat beside the duck pond instead—which I justify by telling myself it's a more genuine appreciation of biology, anyway.

I can't shake the feeling that everything is pointless—that there are mysterious things in the world that might be genuinely interesting, but they're all off-limits—and my mother's erratic anger makes me want to crawl away and hide. Last week she actually looked me in the eye and said, "If I'm unhappy, you're going to be unhappy." Now that he's moved out, she tries to control our interactions with our dad—listening in on phone conversations, dictating what we should say, making us pretend we don't want to see him—and we're not allowed to tell him what really goes on. Perversely, I'm mad at him; it frustrates me that he still bends over backward to meet her demands. I wish my father could temper my mother, but he's a soft-spoken science nerd, and she's a woman on fire.

When I see him for our weekend visit, my father can tell something's wrong. "Care to fill me in on what's happening at school?" he asks once we're settled in a corner booth at the Friendly's in Woburn. My mother must have told him I stayed home sick when I wasn't.

I tear a potato patty in half and toss it on my plate. I'm more in the mood to vandalize my food than to eat it. "Why should I answer your questions when you won't answer mine?"

"When have I ever not answered a question? You may not have always *liked* the answer, but I always try my best to answer you."

He's giving me his open-and-listening look—so earnest, it's embarrassing. I drag a sausage link through a pond of syrup and leave it there to drown. I'd like to tell him about my William Blake conundrum, and my sense that there's a voice whispering in my ear before I fall asleep, but I know he wouldn't get it.

"Do you believe in angels?" I ask.

"No."

"Why not?"

"I just don't. Can we control what we believe? If I told you the earth was flat, could you believe me?"

It's pointless. My father is all logic, all the time. He'll never be able to help me with this.

The day he died, Andrew Cook was playing basketball at the local grammar school when his heart went out of rhythm and just stopped. One of his friends tried to give him mouth-to-mouth, but it didn't work. I wasn't there, but I can see the scene: Andrew, collapsed on his side, wearing his royal blue gym shorts with the white trim. He'd had a slight crush on me, and I hadn't been as nice to him as I could have been—playing dumb the day he tried to figure out how I felt, when I knew perfectly well what he was getting at. Now there's a disturbing urgency to his presence in my dreams.

I turn to face the rain-streaked window. Outside, the cars all have their headlights on; the wet morning is as dark as night.

"What do you think happens when we die?" I ask, staring, I suddenly realize, at my own reflection. My father finishes chewing and swallows before he speaks.

"The body is typically buried, then it decomposes. Everything in nature is interconnected—each death becomes a feast for life."

I start to cry. I can't help it. Tears streak my face, mirroring the rain.

My father lets me cry without interrupting. He thinks feelings should be felt, not stifled. I wipe my nose on the sleeve of my sweatshirt.

"Everything ends, then . . . poof? We just vanish forever from the face of the earth?"

"I want you to be able to trust me," he says, pulling a rough brown napkin from the dispenser and handing it to me. He's waiting for me to take it, but I don't. "Your whole life, I want you to know that you can always come to me and ask me anything, and I'll do my best to give you an honest answer."

I know this speech. It's the same one he gave when I was in third grade. He unhooked a delicate, feathered ornament from the top of the Christmas tree and spoke of tiny songbirds that could fly all the way across the Atlantic without once needing to stop, and computer chips the size of his pinkie nail that contained every letter of every book. Life was too full of fantastical things that were true to justify wasting your mind on fantastical things that were not. He said the same thing then as he says now.

"You don't have to believe in fairy tales. The truth is the greatest miracle there is."

Whatever. The pancakes taste like cardboard, and I shuttle pieces into my napkin when he's not looking. His whole worldview—that knowledge has to be substantiated by repeatable, quantifiable facts—seems ridiculous (what about all the things you can't *prove* but you can *feel?*), and I punish him by clamming up for the rest of the weekend under my Walkman headphones. Usually we make fried dough with ice cream and watch *Saturday Night Live* together, but this weekend, I fake a stomachache and go to bed early so I can read Rupert Sheldrake with a flashlight under the covers. The only problem with having your dad as your best friend is that when you and your dad aren't getting along, you have no one.

MORSE CODE FROM THE DEAD

Maybe life is a painful pilgrimage no one really understands. Maybe we're all alone in the cosmos. When I grow morose and noncommunicative in the weeks that follow, my father makes me go on a school ski trip.

"You'll make friends," he says. "It'll be fun."

"It won't be fun. I don't know how to ski, and I hate everyone."

On the bus, I sit by myself and listen to Foreigner sing "I Want to Know What Love Is" over and over as we pass an endless stretch of cluttered driveways and sad little houses. After a while, the amber glow in the bus works a kind of magic, and I can see how the other kids and I are all riding the same beam of light. I feel connected to them even though I'm alone, which I know is strange; I often feel much less lonely when I'm by myself than I do with other people.

At the hotel, the chaperone puts me in a room with three popular girls who all have matching Dorothy Hamill haircuts and wear scrunched-up leg warmers over their jeans. My hair is pulled back in a sleek strawberry-blond ponytail, and I'm wearing my favorite T-shirt, the one of the Go-Go's waterskiing. It's not a bad outfit, and it seems like I should fit in, but I always worry that my reputation as a good student precedes and discredits me. Before we've been there an hour, ten more kids have shown up, and everyone's sitting on the floor, passing around contraband cans of Schlitz and telling creepy stories. I sit at the far edge of the circle—half in and half out.

"I heard about this kid," says one of the boys, "from another school, who made this *totally awesome* Halloween costume that was, like, *so realistic*. He put a wooden board under his shirt and stuck a knife halfway through it and then covered his shirt with ketchup or spaghetti sauce or something. You know, to look like a stabbing? But then he fell down, and the knife went *all the way in*, and the kid died *for real*."

"That's an urban myth," says one of the girls. "But I know something that's horrifying and *true*. My mom's friend was on a plane to Italy, and her husband went to the bathroom and then didn't come out for a really, really long time. When they broke in the door, the guy had *died* in there. So they brought him back to his seat and buckled him in, and she had to sit next to her husband's dead body for the rest of the flight."

"Oh my God," I say quietly. "*Is* that true?"

"Go ahead and call the FBI if you don't believe me!"

A semicute boy in the corner pulls the tab off a fresh can of beer. He wears the collar of his polo shirt turned up, but his lips are so slick with spit it looks as if he's wearing lip gloss. It's rumored that his parents offered to take him to Jerusalem for his bar mitzvah, but he said he'd rather go to Six Flags.

"If you dial PICKLE with an extra *E* from the 617 area code, it'll connect you with the FBI," he says in a low voice. "I swear—try it."

The story circle moves from there to a discussion of the world's most successful counterfeit operation (bleaching one-dollar bills and reprinting them as hundreds), to Jamie Lee Curtis's sex chromosomes, to disgusting fabrications about the contents of Mick Jagger's stomach. The girls claim eating a spoonful of cinnamon can kill you; the boys say drinking a gallon of Mountain Dew will make your pee glow in the dark.

I don't believe any of it. I'm holding a can of beer, but it's just for show. My mother is a strong believer that drugs and alcohol can ruin your life in one fell swoop—soon, she'll feel completely vindicated yet saddened by what happens to Len Bias—and for the time being, I still heed her warnings.

"It's your turn, Alethea," says one of the boys, kicking the sole of my sneaker with the tip of his shoe.

"My turn what?"

"Tell us a story."

The room goes perfectly quiet—the girl beside me even stops chewing her gum—and I wish myself dead or invisible. I dislike having the attention of multiple people trained on me at once; even the attention of a single person can feel oppressive.

"I don't know any stories," I say, staring down at my beer. I wish I could tell them about Andrew Cook whispering in my ear at night, the inchoate sense I have that he's trying to communicate with me. "Sometimes, late at night . . . I hear things," I mumble.

The girl who brought a Ouija board in her bag leans forward. "Things from the other side?"

"I don't know." I look up. "Maybe."

The boy beside me pounds the cooler like a drum. "You hear *actual voices*? What'd they say?"

Everyone stares. I can feel my face scorching. "What? No, I—nothing."

"Look at her, she's beet red! She turns beet red when she lies!"

"Leave her alone!" says one of the Dorothy Hamill girls.

The boy's smirk has a sexual cast. "Make me."

I walk down the hall to the chaperone's room and ask to call my father.

"I don't feel well," I tell him. "I want to come home."

"You just got there," he says, with authority. "Give it time. It'll get better."

15

But it doesn't get better. My Gore-Tex mittens stiffen my hands like boxing gloves, and in my snowsuit and ski boots, I move like a robotic stuffed animal. For the rest of the weekend, I snowplow down the bunny slope and am dragged back up by a moving rope that I grab for dear life, while the rest of my classmates slalom black diamonds together and ride the chairlift in laughing pairs.

On the bus ride home, I sit with the chaperone instead of with my classmates. The night before, I dreamed of Andrew Cook again. He was underwater, and when his lips moved, instead of words, fish came out. Ever since I woke up, my ears have felt funny. I tilt my head from side to side and bang my temple with the butt of my wrist. When the chaperone asks what's wrong, I say I don't know. "Could it be the changes in altitude?" he asks. I don't want to say no, it feels as though someone's trying to communicate with me, only I have my radio tuned to the wrong station.

When I see my father the following weekend and tell him I think I've started hearing voices, he pretends not to understand.

"It's the power of suggestion," he says. "It's a very common phe-nomenon. You and the other kids were talking about hearing voices. Then you began to imagine you were hearing them."

"We were not!" I say. "We were talking about Jamie Lee Curtis."

I prop my Nikes on his desk to express my displeasure. I don't like coming to work with him anymore; it's boring, when it used to be fun. All the things about math that used to amuse me only aggravate me now, stupid things like *Wiener measure* and the *hairy ball theorem* and the *Cox-Zucker machine*. I make a show of checking my watch.

"Can we go?"

My father doesn't answer but just continues sliding pieces of paper into various files. He claims he spends half his time at work clearing off his desk. I'm waiting for him to wrap it up so the two of us can go to the Lexington track and get takeout crispy beef from Hsin Hsin, our favorite greasy chopstick. I can tell he's trying to think of something for me to do.

In a surprise move, he suggests I record the outgoing message on his answering machine. This I like. It's actually kind of genius. I rub my hands together, lift the lid, and try on different accents. Occasionally, at the office, my father lets me answer his phone for him. Mathematicians from all over the world call on him, but, for some reason, my favorite are the Russians. I like the idea of them—their exotic infused vodkas and tins of delicate silver fish that look like jewelry. Recently, at a math event, a foreign mathematician with scarlet lipstick and a black silk blouse took me aside to confide: "Your father is what we like to call *tragically intelligent.*"

"Is he?" I said. "At home I just call him tragic."

Now, I try on her voice as I push the record button. It takes several attempts, and I have to keep wiping my palms on the front of my jeans, but, eventually, I get it right.

"This is 253-6691. You have reached the office of Fischer Black. No one is in the office at the present time; however, if you leave your name, number, and a brief message, your call will be returned. Start speaking when you hear the tone. Thank you for calling."

After we eat our crispy beef, my father drives me home in the big white whale. We ride in silence, invisibly linked. When he tells me he's going to keep my outgoing message forever, I know it's the truth. Of course he will. He will always work in that office, and that will always be his phone number, and mathematicians will forever hear my fake Russian accent when they call. This isn't the last day I'll ever see him at MIT, or the last time he'll hold two fortune cookies in his closed fists so I can choose my own destiny. This ordinary afternoon, when I'm wearing a pilled gray sweater and my least favorite blue jeans, isn't the end of an era I never realized was ending. My father puts a cassette in the tape deck, and, beneath the song, as he sings along, I know he's trying to tell me something. But I can't hear it. It's too jumbled, too gauzy—too far away.

When he pulls in the driveway and shifts the car into park, I don't get out. This used to be his driveway; he used to live here, too. It doesn't seem right that now he's just a visitor, like someone from another world. He turns off the engine and asks if there's something else I'd like to talk about. There is, but how? *I never see your shoulders beneath the yellow light at the kitchen sink anymore. You left behind your favorite mechanical pencils.* Instead, I sit in the passenger seat, crying.

Eventually, after I slam the door and climb the cement steps, he backs out of the driveway and steers the big white wagon away. I can still see his pale hand waving behind the glass, even after his vehicle vanishes. Inside the house, the air around me whispers; something feels incomplete. I go to the living room, find the rose that's the exact center of the oriental carpet, and sit on it. Somehow I know this is what I'm supposed to do. I'm following secret instructions, and I follow them to a T. Christmas lights on the bushes outside throw their muted hues into the room. I sit in the glowing darkness, eye level with the whispering furniture, staring out at the empty street. For over an hour, I wait on the rose at the center of the carpet, convinced he's going to do it. But my father never comes back for me.

It doesn't make sense. *How could he leave? How could he go away, when he still hasn't explained the nature of all that's hidden, he still hasn't shown me the world's secret things?*

LOVE'S AUSTERE AND LONELY OFFICES

The following year, I stop seeing my father on weekends. A boy in my class has asked me out—a boy who's introverted like me, even though he's also cocaptain of the lacrosse team—and I start spending time with him on weekends instead. For a long while, I forget about my interest in angels and auras and the layers of reality that exclude the senses. Every Tuesday afternoon, I go to John's games. I like to sit in the bleachers with the other friends and girlfriends of the players. All the cliques who'd been snotty to me start being nice when John and I begin dating, and, once they embrace me, I try to pretend I was wrong about them all along.

My father still keeps some of my clothes in a dresser in his rented room in Arlington. One of the last times I visit him there, I walk downstairs to find him sitting at the breakfast table, wearing his calm-but-ecstatic face. He's toasted a round blueberry waffle and set it at my place. I linger on the bottom step.

"I'm not that into breakfast these days," I say. "I'm on a diet."

His expression shifts, but he stops short of sharing his thoughts on dieting. "That's all right. We can just sit and talk. Enjoy each other's company."

"My ride's going to be here in five minutes." It's the first warm day of spring, and the En Ka Fair is in town. John and I are going to double-date with two of his friends. "I have to curl my hair."

"How 'bout I give you a ride?"

"Dad," I say, turning on my heel and heading back upstairs. "Are you even *serious*?"

I tell myself he doesn't change; he just gets a little absentminded, a little distracted as he ages—it happens to everyone. And I mostly believe it. He forgets where he put the car keys; he searches for the right word; he walks into a room and can't remember why he's there. He tries to make a joke of it—"Do *you* remember why I came in here?"—but I can tell it bothers him. Even though he goes to bed early, he'll sometimes nod off midsentence. One day he can't recall the name of our next-door neighbor and friend, the one he's always liked so much. He calls her Emily, but her name is Elizabeth.

The two of us drift apart quietly and without fanfare, until one day I lift my head, stop curling my hair, and shift my gaze for a split second off John and leg warmers and the glittering distractions of my high school life, and he's gone. When he decides to leave MIT for an investment-banking job in New York, he doesn't tell me himself—I first hear about it from my mother.

Before he moves away, there's a special day, when he'll teach his last class and everyone will wish him farewell. I've made plans to meet him at his office after school, but when I get to school, I discover there's a playoff game for the lacrosse tournament that afternoon. I'm too ashamed to tell him I want to go to that instead, so I just don't show. And don't call. We never speak of it—he never brings it up, and I never apologize—and, ultimately, as the decades pass, when I think back to this moment, this adolescent moment, I know it was just one day in my life, one afternoon, more than thirty years ago. But when I think of him now, I don't remember his face in the lamplight at the entrance to my room, or the sound of his voice reading to me, or even those images of him in hospice at the end—his spectral self as he slipped into space. I think of him sitting alone at his desk on his special day, squaring a stack of paper, waiting for the daughter who never arrives. The clock on the wall ticks off the minutes; the answering machine at his elbow holds my coiled voice. I've listened to that message so many times that, even all these years later, I still have his office number in my head.

It's a gusty October afternoon when I decide to call. All week, the wind has been whispering. Every time I spin around, the brown leaves swirl in circles. It's in these haunting autumn afternoons, beneath the surface currents of life, that I've sensed a deeper truth: my father isn't gone; he's here, and he still has something to tell me. I'm surprised to see my fingers tremble as I dial, as I hear the old chant of the numerals, its familiar music—a summoning. I tuck the phone against my shoulder and unconsciously hold my breath. But of course no one answers.

PART II

YOU, ON A GOOD DAY

You don't give the finger to the black pickup truck that tailgates and passes you aggressively, then let go of the wheel to give it two fingers when you see a rainbow-colored peace sticker on its bumper. You do not call the friend—the one who was in the hospital a few weeks ago, whom you did not visit or call— you do not call her today, because today you need something from her. You do not consider dousing your refrigerator with gasoline and setting it on fire because of the sound its compressor makes while you're trying to work. You do not wish the earth would just ignite and get it over with simply because it's been hot for a few days. You do not conjure up, in as vivid detail as possible, every time anyone has ever wronged you in any way. You do not think: *We're a ruined, useless lot, and we deserve everything we get.* You do not say under your breath, while refusing to let yourself smoke a pack of cigarettes: "It's either pain in the body or pain in the mind. Take your pick."

In church, after the sermon, you do not wonder aloud: *Where's Lazarus now? Dead again. That's where.* You do not spot the white-haired lady who always brings up politics in order to let you know that your politics are all wrong and think: *You ignorant, arrogant, self-righteous old hag.* Later on, when you pass the Trader Joe's clerk who seems dispirited by your very presence, you do not think: *You have no use for me? Well, guess what? I have no use for you, either.* You do not realize, as you think this, that this is a phrase—"to have no use for"—that you have acquired from your mother. As you exit, when the excessively cheerful clerk says: "Have a nice day!" you do not say: "I'm afraid I already have other plans." You do not consider telling the French-braided girl in the parking lot who looks just like you would have looked as a child, if you had ever been a child: "Get out now, while you still can."

While driving to the hair salon, you do not think of your neighbor's teenage son who got drunk and then got behind the wheel and killed himself and four of his friends. In the shampooing chair, you do not ask why all retail establishments cool themselves to minus 70 Kelvin in the summer so that a person has to be miserable both outside and inside. You do not say to your hairdresser, as she scrubs your scalp so enthusiastically that you wonder if you're starting to bleed: "I just washed it this morning, and I haven't been rolled in tar since then."

You do not wish that your hairdresser would stop talking about her near-death experiences and start focusing on what she's doing with the scissors. You do not care more about your bangs than you do about the life of a sister human. As your hairdresser continues to talk about death and dismemberment, you do not think about the doctor who told your friend, the one you did not call, that the lump in her breast was just a cyst. You do not imagine your friend's face beneath the green-and-yellow scarf where her hair used to be.

When you get home, you do not let the fact that your Internet connection has gone out make you want to eat your own hands. You do not tell the girl on the other end of the phone line that she and her Comcast friends have picked the wrong day to mess with you. You do not feel fury at yourself when the Comcast man arrives, hours later, and it turns out the problem was that your modem was on standby and all you had to do was push a little black button that you had, in fact, already pushed, several times, but apparently not in the right way. You do not tell the Comcast man who knows how to push your buttons that, for some reason, all technological devices hate you; it's mystifying, you have never done a single thing to them.

You do not sit at your desk and think about the president you did not like and that other president you did not like and all the things they did that you did not like. You do not think about sleazy televangelists and sexual harassers. When the phone rings and your friend is upset because her eighty-eight-year-old father is terminally ill, you do not calculate, in your mind, how many more years she's gotten to have a father than you did. You do not think about your other friend, the one who likes to complain that everyone else is successful because they came from money and their parents helped them, and she isn't successful because she didn't come from money and her parents never helped her. You do not wish you'd said to her: "Keep telling yourself that." You do not think about the beautiful barn swallow that flew into your window and died.

You do not fix yourself a hamburger and feel rage at the friend who lectures you about vitamin D and omega-3s and fish-farming and how you should eat only animals that are free range, grass fed, and given a daily massage and, actually, it'd be best if you had all your food shipped to you on dry ice from a Mennonite farm in Arkansas, because that's the way she does it. You do not recall the day you said to her: "Please don't tell me anything bad about coffee, because coffee is the only reliable source of pleasure in my daily life," and she said: "Coffee is one of the most heavily pesticided crops on the planet." You do not think about telling her, again, that you don't care. And you do not wonder, since she's a little hard of hearing, if maybe you should just make a giant cardboard sign to wear the next time you see her that reads "I DON'T CARE." You do not think about reminding her that you ate Froot Loops every day of your life for the first ten years, so if it's a little corn-fed chicken that does you in, so be it. You do not consider telling her that you do not want your whole life to be about food—that your whole life *was* about food for many sad years, and now you're ready for it to be about something else.

You do not remember the guy who mused aloud on your first and final date whether he was more of a "leg man" or a "breast man." You do not wish, again, that you'd told him you were a "dick woman."

You do not think about the spring day your neighbor's teenage son, who later got drunk and got behind the wheel, visited your house with his sister when he was still a six-year-old boy. You do not remember how he took you aside to confide: "My penis has powers," and how you tried so hard not to laugh, you almost burst a blood vessel. You do not ponder how strange it is that your neighbor's teenage son went from being a four-foot little boy to a six-foot young man while you were living next door and, in that same time period, you did not change at all. You do not contemplate how you have never been young and you will never be old because you have always been just this, this voice.

You do not avoid doing your freelance work that is already past its deadline anyway to write an ex-boyfriend a letter. You do not say in this letter everything that you could have said when you broke up with him—everything you dislike about him—even though he begged at the time to be told what it was you disliked about him. You did not do so then because you are too nice, and a coward, plus you did not see the point in insulting a person if there's nothing beneath the insults that you want to keep. But now, you write out everything you disliked about him, in longhand.

You did not like the way he always wanted to talk to you in the car when you would have preferred to listen to a book on tape sometimes. You did not like the way he always wanted to talk to you when you were trying to write your emails. You did not like the way he always wanted to talk to you while you were in the shower—the toilet is meant for sitting on and doing your business, not sitting on with the lid down while you talk to the person who is trying to take a shower in private.

Maybe all the talking would have been all right if the things that were said had been more interesting. Maybe. But—maybe not. Also, the frequency with which he released certain emissions from the ass in your presence: you did not like that. You realize that sometimes these things need to happen in the presence of another person, and you'd even consider a small amount of that to be a kind of compliment. But this order of magnitude was no compliment and, in fact, may have indicated some sort of dietary adjustment was in order. Also, he didn't love something else enough—something other than you.

You do not think about the men you've known in your twenty-five years of knowing men. You do not think about the one who told you that "uninhibited" was an awfully long word to be using at three in the morning, so, in turn, you offered him four short words: "cock, pussy, me, you." You do not think about the one who wanted to own you and keep you in a little cage, who wanted you to give up your name—your father's name—and take his name instead. You do not think about the one who drank Guinness with you before a movie on a Sunday afternoon and when you said you wanted to order a chicken sandwich and stick it in your purse in case you got hungry during the film acted as if this were the most bizarre thing he had ever heard of or could imagine. You do not think of how you knew right then that it was doomed, because, honestly, if he couldn't handle your chicken, how could he handle the rest of you? You do not think *I only really love the broken ones, the ones who can't or won't love me back.*

You do not feel as if your breasts are swollen; you do not feel as if your womb is swollen; you do not feel as if your head and heart are swollen.

You do not go outside and walk the streets in despair—the same despair you've been aware of for as long as you can remember. You do not think of your college lover who told you: "If you dig deep enough, you're always going to hit that sadness. That sadness is like the water table."

You do not think about the short, ugly guy all your college classmates used to call Weasel and how you went up to them in the dining hall one day and asked them to please stop calling him Weasel because it was not his real name, and even though he pretended to embrace it and even kind of like it, you couldn't believe he truly did, and besides, his real name was actually quite beautiful, so maybe they could try using his real name for a change. You do not think about how later that week, when they put Weasel up to asking you to the winter formal, even though you did not have a date or someone else you wanted to go with, you said no.

You do not come home, drink a bottle of wine, and feel that you could easily drink another. You do not smoke the pack of cigarettes that you promised yourself you wouldn't smoke but nevertheless failed to run under the faucet before you threw them away. You do not hear a song by Simply Red and say: "I hated this song in 1989, and I hate it even more now." You do not think of the word *webinar*. You do not think, whenever someone calls you, *This person just wants something from me*. You do not contemplate the myriad ways in which you have been defeated, manipulated, deceived, and abused. You do not feel a desire both to consume and be consumed. You do not ask, of your own marrow, *What is this fire?* You do not lie in your bed with your fists clenched and howl in the dark at nothing.

You do not remember how your neighbor's teen-age son, who later got drunk and got behind the wheel, looked when he was just a boy and he and his sister used to come to your house to draw with watercolor pencils and bake banana-bread muffins. You do not think about the day he picked up the rock on your desk with the word *WISDOM* on it and asked what *WISDOM* meant. You do not remember that you said it meant things that were deeply true, or something like that, and his sister said: "Like, don't pick your nose when you're outside," and how the three of you proceeded to play a game called "That's

Wisdom!" where one person would shout: "Don't water the plants with your peeper!" or "Bugs taste better with ketchup and mustard!" and the other two would shout: "That's wisdom!" in unison. You do not recall how he told you that you and your dog were his favorite people on planet Earth and you were better than any of his friends. You do not wonder if he or any of his friends had been conscious when the car caught fire. You do not think of the black scorched scar in the tree.

In the middle of the night, when you can't sleep, you do not get up and go for a walk and try to remember who it was that said in New York City you could walk the streets weeping, bleeding, and naked and still be invisible. You do not try to think of one purely selfless act that you have ever done in your life and come up empty. You do not think: *Somewhere along the way, we lost it. We lost the capacity for real love.* You do not stare up at the sky, at the place where the stars should be, and see nothing. You do not keep standing there and staring, like an idiot, like a child, as if you expect the stars are going to suddenly appear. You do not think: *It's over. It's ruined. We had our chance, and we missed it.*

You do not, you do not, you do not.

Not on this day. On this day, you wake up remembering the sight of your friend's four-year-old son aiming all his fire trucks at the TV during coverage of 9/11 because he wanted to help. On this day, you think about the afternoon you heard a famous poet thoughtfully, lovingly, gently answer a deranged question from an audience member who was mentally ill. On this day, you think about the time the woman in the ATM vestibule beside yours heard you crying on the customer-service phone because you'd pushed the wrong button and you needed access to that money right away, because that check was all the money you had, and she'd reached into her wallet and handed you a twenty. On this day, you think about the cameramen you heard about, the ones who were filming a rape trial, and crying. On this day, you remember Anne Frank's scribbled little words—or you don't so much remember them as you see them floating before your eyes, because you've got them taped to your wall—"It's a wonder I haven't abandoned all my ideals, they seem so absurd and impractical. Yet I cling to them because I still believe, in spite of everything, that people are truly good at heart."

On this day, you go to Central Park and watch a row of ducklings and their mother waddle across a path. On this day, you see the one in the back, who's having a hard time keeping up with the rest, because it looks as if there may be something wrong with its foot, or its little yellow head, and you think: *That's me.* On this day, you think: *It isn't all rot. There's some goodness left somewhere, a tiny fleck of it, maybe around the eyes or the mouth or on the teeth, like a stray piece of spinach.* On this day, you remember hurt people hurt people. On this day, you think: *We're all just trying to get through this thing*. On this day, you think about the word *ukulele*. In church, you think: *He loves us, and he died for us*.

On this day, you remember your high school science teacher, the one who told you that fate was like a carousel and if you miss your horse the first time it comes around, or even the first, second, third, fourth, and fifth times—if you're a person who's really good at missing things—it will come around for you again. On this day, you remember the friend who comforted you by saying: "If it's meant to be, you can't ruin it," and "All you need is for one little thing to go right, and everything else can flow from that one little thing."

On this day, you remember—because you remember now how often you remember things wrong—that the barn swallow *didn't* die. You thought it was dead, but then it got up and flew away.

On this day, while walking through the city, you take a different turn, on an impulse, and walk down Lafayette Street. And this different turn makes you remember the last time you walked down Lafayette

Street, at four o'clock in the morning after a really great election-night party in 2008. And you remember how you were really drunk that night, because at the really great election-night party, you had gotten into a tremendous fight with your boyfriend—the one who'd wanted you to take his name—and you had yelled something about how you didn't want to be owned by anyone, you didn't want to participate in the ownership society, the society of people owning other people, and why did it have to be that way, anyway? Oh, yeah, because there was no such thing as real love, or maybe there was, but human beings didn't seem capable of it anymore, if they ever had been.

And you remember how, at four in the morning on that night in 2008, as you stumbled down Lafayette, there'd been a guy on a skateboard who zoomed past you, riding in the middle of the vacant street and trailing a thirty-foot-long American flag. And you remember how that flag seemed to billow for blocks, how it was the most stunning, most magnificent American flag you'd ever seen, and how, even though you're not a person who is particularly moved by flags, tears sprang to your eyes as this billowing vision of stars and stripes moved past you and through you and overtook you. And you remember how it felt as though you were watching a scene from a movie and you wished there'd been other people there to see it, too.

On this day, the remembrance of the skateboarding American flag that was just like a scene from the movies makes you want to go to the movies, so you do. You go on a whim, as always. You just sort of show up at a theater and see what's playing, because you're either too lazy or too freedom loving to plan things in advance. This strategy of moviegoing does not tend to work out well for you, but on this day, something is playing that you've actually been wanting to see. So you buy a Kit Kat and find a seat in the back and put your feet up.

On this day, a few rows in front of you, a couple is sharing a soda, passing it back and forth and forth and back, being kind. Their kindness makes you want to go over and give them something, maybe one of your Kit Kats, but you don't, because the movie is starting. The movie is set in the 1970s and is about secrets and grace and the mysterious ways we are called to bear with one another. In addition to being good, it's beautiful. And it's nostalgic for you, all the 1970s cars and the 1970s sidewalks and the 1970s light. You had not thought it possible to capture sunlight from a particular era on film, but apparently it is, because all of a sudden you remember that you *were* a child once, and it must have been in the 1970s, because you remember walking around in that light. You're halfway through the movie when you discover that you're crying, which is strange, because it isn't even a sad movie. You're crying because it's good.

On this day, when the movie ends, the other people get up and file out of the theater, talking and chewing their gum, as if they haven't just been present at a miracle. Because that's the way it always is: first, miracle, then: time to make the chicken. But on this day, you don't get up. You don't get up because you don't want it to be over. So you continue to sit there, silently holding your Kit Kat wrapper in your seat at the back, long after the music has stopped and the lights have come on and everyone else has gone home.

REASON TO STAY

Before he dies, my father tells me he isn't afraid, he's had a good life, his only fear is that he's letting me down. This is in June—on Father's Day—and he will die at his home in New Canaan a little over eight weeks later. His cancer of the base of the tongue / floor of the mouth is already stage four when they find it, and when he calls and tells me the news in a soft, halting voice, he delivers both punches at once: "I have cancer. It's terminal."

My father is holding my hand when he says he isn't afraid and when he asks, with his mathematical mind, if I know why it is that people have to die. I press my lips and shake my head; speech is not available to me.

"To make room for the babies," he says. Then he gives my fingers a squeeze. *Don't be afraid,* the squeeze is saying. *I'm letting you see, so you'll remember this someday. It's all okay.*

But it *isn't* all okay. I've been staying at my father's house for a couple of weeks, now that he's home from the hospital and is in the hospice phase.

When he tells me he's worried about me, I try to reassure him that I have everything under control. I attempt some lie. I act casual while I tell the lie—I touch my ear; I scratch at a mustard stain on my jeans. This is a performance. Everything is a performance. I don't tell him that I often stay up all night and sleep all day, that I've stopped paying my bills and doing laundry, that the IRS would like to speak with me. I don't tell him that I fail to understand where other people get the strength to lead their lives. I *definitely* don't tell him about the eating disorder I've developed that flushes buckets of money down the toilet each night and takes up huge amounts of my spare time—although, I have no job, so, really, all my time is spare. I don't tell him there's a reason I ride the bus and go to the movies: I'm waiting for the world to give me a reason to stay.

My father knows all this, of course. He's my father. He knows everything. But I can't discuss it with him, because I don't know how to explain it. If I'm depressed, I've been depressed my whole life. Whenever I see an infant wailing inconsolably, as if she's confused, as if she does not want this life or understand why she's been thrown into it, I feel a stab of recognition, as if she's wailing for me.

My father, my hero, my closest friend, continues to die before my eyes. I try to witness his deterioration with courage. I get out of bed. I walk around. I say things. But this is a lie. It's all a lie.

"I'm worried about you," he continues to whisper, even when the light grows dim and his voice begins to fail.

When he dies, I hide in a closet, so no one can find me when they come to put his body in a bag. I don't want to see his body without him in it.

If things were bad while he was passing away, they become even worse after he's gone. I've graduated from college, but I don't know what to do with my life. I have a little money from my father, so I mope along, trying to figure things out. During the day, I wander the streets of Manhattan in a trance, half floating above the pavement. Sometimes I ride the M104 bus all the way to the end of the line and back, staring out the window at the city scenes. I like riding the bus. It perfectly embodies how I feel: part of the world but also separate from it. I eat toasted Reubens in steamy diners, with my face in a book, and when I'm feeling downhearted, which is often, I go to the movies on the Upper West Side. I prefer the old theater that has homemade brownies and an escalator that plunges us all underground. While I watch the picture, my eyes glued to the screen, I have the sense that I'm looking for something, but I don't know what. After several mediocre movies in a row, I decide that whatever I'm searching for, it's not Vince Vaughn.

After procrastinating for months, I finally make an appointment with a grief counselor. I get the counselor's name from the bartender who works at the pub on the corner. The bartender's brother killed himself, and the bartender, who is attractive, sometimes refills my wineglass for free. These things conspire to make me willing to try his therapist, even though, generally speaking, I'm deeply suspicious of therapy.

The day of my appointment, I wake up at two in the afternoon. My appointment is scheduled for two in the afternoon. As usual, I was up the night before until the sun rose, and I must have slept through my alarm. Oh, wait: I don't have an alarm, which might be part of the problem. I scramble out of "bed," which is a mattress on the floor of a basement apartment owned by my uncle, and sniff the clothes that are strewn about, trying to decide which are cleanest. It feels odd to be sniffing my underwear—it's not the most empowered way to start my day—but I do so out of respect for my future therapist. I suspect that if our roles were reversed, she'd do the same for me.

My future therapist's office is on Lexington Avenue, and I could take the bus. That route is covered by the M103, a line I love; sometimes I ride that bus up and back and then eat a pastrami sandwich at the Lenox Hill Grill and play with the puppies at Pets on Lex. But today, I'm in a hurry—there's no time for puppies or pastrami. I have to take a cab.

I arrive at my future therapist's office fifty-five minutes late. She ushers me in briskly, and the first thing I see is a shelf of religious figurines—there's a wooden Jesus, a glass Gandhi, and a Buddha made of jade. I'm not 100 percent certain the glass one is Gandhi; it could be Golda Meir.

My future therapist gives me a big, bright smile, even though nothing joyful has happened. She, too, is performing. She sits in a tall leather chair behind a desk. From the window to her left, slanted sunlight falls on the figurines, revealing dust on the Buddha's belly. My future therapist speaks to me, telling me a little about herself, her professional approach. She seems open; she seems genuinely interested in hearing all the things I never say. If I were ready, these are some of the things I might tell her: *I'm not sure why I'm here, I don't like it here, I don't understand it here, and I don't want to be here.*

At the end of her little speech, she stops. I know that's my cue to talk, but as soon as I open my mouth, tears pour out of my eyes. I remain in full waterfall mode for about five minutes, which is all the time I have left. I am, in fact, still crying when a little alarm on my grief counselor's desk goes *bing!*

So my attempt at grief counseling is a failure. There's grief, but there is no counseling, and I can do grief at home, for free. Even though the bartender is cute, and my future therapist seems nice, I know I'll never see her again. At the time, I tell myself I'm not ready. I don't realize that, often, by the time you're ready for something, you don't need it anymore.

A few weeks later, I wake from a dream with a vivid sense of purpose. I know what I need to do. I need to get a job, to make my father proud.

I love movies—the ones without Vince Vaughn in them—so I apply to be a ticket taker at the movie theater I like, near Lincoln Center. When my cab pulls up on the day of my interview, I search frantically in my purse for the fare. I could have gotten the fare ready while the cab was still moving, before it came to a complete stop in the middle of traffic with twelve cars behind it, but that was when I was putting on my makeup. Now, in my rush, I spill my change purse on the floor. Coins and bills scatter everywhere, and I swear under my breath as I get down and grope around for my money. It's sticky and dirty and dark there on the floor of the cab, and I collect the bills but leave the coins because I don't have time for that; I can't be groveling for change out here when I'm supposed to be groveling in the theater. I make a split-second decision that I should leave a one-dollar bill on the floor of the cab, along with the change, so the cabbie won't be fishing around on his hands and knees for just pennies, which seems sort of degrading. But I don't have a dollar, so I have to leave him a five, which I kind of hide under the floor mat to keep the next passenger from seeing and seizing it, and I realize, as I carefully do this bizarre thing, that it takes a special sort of person to find a way to actually lose money in becoming employed.

I slam the cab door and check my watch, cursing again, again the victim of my lack of an alarm clock. If only I were still in contact with my future therapist, I might ask her where she got that cunning little device that made such a pleasing yet authoritative *bing*.

Adjacent to the box-office cubicle where I will perhaps soon work, there are two glass display cases. The one on the right is filled with lingerie, and the one on the left is filled with baby clothes, and as I dash past, I think, as I always do: *Before . . . after!*

I arrive at the interview panting a little, sweating in my semiclean underwear, trailing my purse with its crumpled bills and a hairy hairbrush sticking out. But, in spite of all this, the interview goes well. Even though they did not ask me to, I've worn black pants and a white shirt, to look the part. I don't own a bow tie, but I've clipped a black hair bow through the top buttonhole of my collar, as an approximation.

The interviewer, a middle-aged woman named Roberta, asks me about movies, and this is where things really pick up. I love movies. I see them all the time. I believe the unmasked heart of the universe might exist in a movie somewhere; I just haven't seen it yet. When she asks me which movies I love, my mind goes blank, and I have to root around in my memory for a second, because sometimes when I'm asked something directly like that, I get nervous, and the answer flies away. My brain alights on that movie I saw here just the other day. *What was it again?* A beat goes by. Another beat.

"*Pulp Fiction!*" I say, and the woman doesn't say anything, so I figure it's still my turn. The only problem with *Pulp Fiction*, I tell her, was that I kept laughing when no one else was laughing, and then, when everyone else was laughing, sometimes I wanted to cry. For instance, that scene when Uma Thurman overdoses. I found that to be very upsetting and stressful. I did not think that was funny at all, yet everyone in the theater was laughing maniacally while I worried for her life and wondered why none of the bozos on-screen were doing something more to help her.

The middle-aged interviewer nods. The interview does not go on much longer after that.

On my way out, I buy a brownie at the concession stand. The sugar lifts me like a drug, and as I hit a bitter nugget of walnut, already I know that later that night, in the privacy of my basement apartment, I'll consume an entire box of brownies, plus a quart of Baskin-Robbins rocky-road ice cream.

\ few days later, I learn that the movie theater does not want to hire me. They send me a rejection letter in the mail, which I save. I actually tie it to a piece of string and dangle it from the fan above my mattress, so I can look at it whenever I want. For some reason, I think it's hilarious. I think it must represent the absolute nadir in the history of something. Perhaps this is the lowest moment of my life. Then again, maybe it's just another slip in a long, downward slide.

In college, I was a Tasti D-Lite girl, so I already know how to swivel my wrist to make shapely chocolate-and-vanilla ice-cream cones. Only Tasti D-Lite isn't ice cream; it's something else, for skinny people who don't want to eat ice cream. Whatever it is, there's a Tasti D-Lite a few blocks from my apartment, and I still need a job.

I pop by the Tasti D-Lite on a Thursday afternoon in my black-and-white getup—just because—forcing a smile even though I think I might pass out from the PTSD that's being brought on by the smell of artificial hazelnut. I wait patiently amid the low hum of the machines, and, eventually, a guy in charge comes out from a back room to inform me that they already have six girls to work three shifts, but that I'm welcome to check back later, if I like, in the spring.

Two strikes is about all I have in me, so I go back to riding the bus. It's nearing Christmas, and a busy time of year for bus riding. The streets are clotted with shoppers, the store windows crammed with elegantly wrapped boxes and stuffed animals that look lonely when our eyes meet. Last Christmas, my father enrolled me in a fruit-of-the-month club. All the notes said the same thing: "FRUIT STIMULATES CREATIVITY!" I wasn't really doing anything creative at the time, but maybe he thought I had potential.

He died before the subscription was through. When I received the first posthumous box of apples, I understood immediately what was going on, but, still, there was something poignant about it—there was that millisecond where my body forgot what my mind knew, and there I was, holding a beribboned box from my dad, a pleasantly hefty package, signed with his words, in his name, as if time were a lie and he was alive again.

To give myself the illusion of making money, I decide to sell some of my possessions. I take the M15 downtown to Stuyvesant and pawn a couple of Billy Joel CDs to the guys displaying things on blankets outside Around the Clock. Then I take the money they give me and buy myself dinner at Around the Clock, where they scoop the carrot-ginger dressing out of an industrial-size vat. They have to make a ton of it every day because everyone in the neighborhood knows it's just that good.

On my way home, I get off the bus one stop early and amble into the Love's pharmacy over on Broadway. It's midnight, the time of day when I'm most alert; this is my peak-performance hour. I move through the store methodically, aisle by aisle, stalking it like a cat. It's not that I think I'm going to find something critically vital for life on earth inside a Love's. But I might.

In aisle five, I spot a sleep mask, which could be useful. Sometimes the morning sun hurts my eyes so much it makes me wonder if I'm descended from a branch of humanity that gave rise to the vampire myths. The sleep mask is satiny and purple and smells of lavender, which I like so much that I walk through the rest of the store holding it beneath my nose like a fake moustache.

In the stationery aisle, there's a Trapper Keeper with a picture of a baby in an elephant costume on it. It could be the influence of the lavender, but, for some reason, this strikes me as supremely useful. I add it to my basket. The expression on the baby's face makes me happy, and suddenly I'm in one of those moods that come over me every once in a while, where I begin to think that maybe—just maybe—I'll be able to forge a life on earth after all.

Buoyed by my newfound sense of possibility, with the Trapper Keeper in my basket, I proceed with caution to the aisle where they sell alarm clocks. I tentatively pick one up. It has a black folded cord dangling behind it like a tail. There's a sticker with red digital numerals on it, displaying a fake time of 6:46.

Six forty-six is a terrible time to be conscious. Nothing good happens at 6:46. Suddenly, I'm imagining all sorts of unpleasant sounds coming out of this thing at that time, startling me awake when I'd rather be sleeping, and, as my gaze shifts from my silky sleep mask to my shiny Trapper Keeper, to this black instrument with the devil numbers on its face, I realize something: I don't own an alarm clock because I don't want to own an alarm clock. I resent alarm clocks. I think they represent a subtle form of slavery, keeping humans from their wildest dreams and deepest sleep. I put the ugly slave master back on its shelf.

In aisle twelve, there's a makeup remover on sale that I like. It's eight dollars if I buy a pack of six or five dollars if I buy a pack of three. But the containers in the three-pack are 4.2 ounces, whereas the containers in the six-pack are only 3.9 ounces, which means . . . well, it means I probably have enough left in my bottle at home.

My lack of aptitude for math always amuses me, because my father wrote an equation that won the Nobel Prize in 1997. He didn't personally win the prize, because it isn't awarded posthumously, but they gave it to his coauthors, who said nice things about my dad when they won. While my father was still alive, in 1994, word got out that he was on the short list for the Nobel that year, and one of his colleagues asked if he wanted him to call up the Royal Swedish Academy of Sciences and inform them that he was terminally ill. My father's answer was something along the lines of: *If you do anything remotely like that, I'll kill you myself.* So it went to John Nash that year, and by the time they honored my father's work, he was dead. That's just the way the cookie crumbled—no use feeling bad about it. Besides, he was never motivated by awards; he always said the greatest reward was the work itself.

As I proceed homeward from Love's, enjoying the relative calm of the wee hours of the morning, I pass by the antiques and greeting-card shop where the gypsy woman read my palm and said I was going to be famous. I didn't buy it; I knew she was just trying to get me to buy a "lucky" moon-rock ring—which I did buy, so I guess her little strategy worked. When she told me the ring was lucky, I said, "Oh, good! I could use a little luck!" but the gypsy woman fixed me with a sharp stare and held up a mirror. "You've been so lucky already," she said.

I'm still feeling hopeful and buoyant when I get to my building, my Trapper Keeper bag in one hand and my scented-sleep-mask bag in the other. As soon as I step through the breezeway, I'm mugged. A wiry teenager in a hooded sweatshirt rushes me from behind as I'm unlocking the second door, and, before I understand what's happening, he jabs me in the back and grabs my purse. Out of some potentially lethal combination of stupidity, instinct, and outrage, I fight him for it. When he wins, I run screaming after him. I call the police. While they take down my description of the guy, I eye their guns. Voices crackle out of their walkie-talkies menacingly. I tell them the assault felt more startling than truly dangerous—that I'd be shocked if the guy actually had any sort of weapon; he just seemed like a strung-out kid. After only a few minutes, they locate my discarded, empty purse in some bushes down the street and return it to me.

Only much later, when the shock has worn off and I'm safely consuming a quart of coconut ice cream with Famous Chocolate Wafers in bed, do I begin to feel bad for that kid, my mugger. Imagine being so desperate that you nerve yourself up to steal from a lonely girl at two in the morning, and then, out of all the possibilities in the world, you pick the one person in this part of Manhattan who has nothing in her purse but a bus pass, a notebook, and Virginia Woolf's diary.

A PLACE IN THE WORLD

After my mugging, I stay in my apartment for a while, holed up like a mouse. Lucky for me, I have enough instant oatmeal, spicy canned chili, and Cinnamon Toast Crunch to last for decades, because there was an earthquake across the country, in California, a few weeks ago, and I like to be prepared. Remaining in a small, confined space suits me. It feels cozy. Some days, I run to the greengrocer on the corner, buy a hunk of cheese, and run back, just to really explore the mouselike feelings. As the weeks pass, I slowly find myself venturing farther and farther afield, which isn't progress, exactly, but more a kind of forgetting.

A couple of months later, I'm riding a bus crammed with people, a hulking, arthritic bus that strains its way up the avenue, when I pass by my future therapist's office. I locate her window and try to catch a glimpse of the shelf of figurines or the profile of some other woebegone person humiliating herself. For some reason I feel drawn to get off a block later, without a clear purpose.

I walk around aimlessly for a while. Then, rounding a corner, I see it. *The Lighthouse: Dedicated to helping people of all ages overcome the challenges of vision loss.* And, just like that, I know. Reading to the blind—that'd be the *perfect* job. I love to read, and I often feel blind, as though the real truth of the world were hidden from me.

The Lighthouse interviewer bears an uncanny resemblance to my future therapist, but she does not give me the big, bright smile my future therapist did. I try not to take it personally. She may be used to working with the visually impaired.

She's holding a copy of my résumé, and her expression is stern.

"What makes you think you're qualified for this job?" she asks.

"I can read," I say.

She says nothing.

"And . . . I like blind people. I mean, I like all people—some people just happen to be blind."

Her brow furrows as she examines me more closely, letting her eyes roam over my person. She seems especially interested in my hair-ribbon bow tie.

The silence is uncomfortable. I feel that one of us should say something.

"Did you know that Helen Keller's favorite foods were hot dogs and martinis?" I have no idea why I say this. The words just come out of my mouth.

It turns out the Lighthouse does not want to hire me, either.

All three of my sisters are worried about me, so one of them, who lives in California, offers to help me get a job. *Come visit,* she says. *Sister function!* She'll polish my résumé—the two of us can drink sangria and brainstorm together. It sounds good, but I'm reluctant because of the transportation issue. I hate to fly, which is too bad, because being way up high in the clouds could be really peaceful and celestial, and I wish I were the kind of person who could enjoy it. Unfortunately, I'm the kind of person who, as soon as the plane hits a little speed bump, starts to cry and asks the stranger next to me if it'd be all right if I held his hand or maybe sat in his lap for a second. Still, I haven't seen my sister in a while, and I need to find something to do with my life, so I stare fear in the face and book a flight.

It's a night flight, and there've been so many weather delays that when the plane finally gets off the ground, the pilot comes over the speaker to apologize for the late start and say that he's going to put the "pedal to the metal" to make up for lost time.

I don't know why pilots are allowed to talk. Nothing a pilot says ever makes me feel good. Whether they say: "Well, folks, sorry for the delay. We just had a few mechanical problems with the plane, but we're *pretty* sure we've got them all ironed out now," or "We'll be taking off just as soon as we can get someone out here to deice the wings again; you all know what'll happen if we don't take off with freshly deiced wings," or "Air traffic has informed us we'll be flying through several small tornados on our way to St. Louis, but don't worry about it." I wish pilots would keep these sentiments to themselves. When a pilot tells me he's going to put the "pedal to the metal," what I hear is: "Not only are you thirty thousand feet above the earth in a rickety tin can that was built in 1980, but hang on to your hats, folks. Cuz I'm going to be speeding."

As the plane gains altitude, I adopt my standard in-flight posture, which is to be extremely nice but not so nice as to invite human communication of any kind. True, I may have to hold someone's hand later. But we'll get to that when we get to it.

They used to have terrific food on airplanes in the 1970s, when I was in grade school and my parents would occasionally put me on a flight to visit my grandparents in Tampa. But the food on airplanes is terrible now, plus I always have some strange, new healthy-eating strategy, so I let the snack cart pass me by, and once it's gone, I reach into my carry-on and remove something totally normal and not at all odd smelling, such as three bunless hamburger patties and a stack of raw onions. I forgot to stash a plate or a knife in there, but no worries—I have my empty plastic cup and a plastic fork. That's all I really need.

Throughout the flight, the announcements from the cockpit keep coming. He's a talker, this pilot. If this were a day flight, he'd be one of the ones who talk about all the stuff on the ground that you can't see. Tonight, he's forced to talk about the weather. First, he lets us know that we're about to hit "a little chop," then "a little turbulence," then "a *lot* of turbulence." Each time, he lets us know the bad thing is coming a minute or so in advance, so we can have that extra moment of fear. I'm just becoming accustomed to his narrative style when . . . I don't know what happens, exactly, except to say that we must have flown right into a storm, because all of a sudden we're lurching up and down so violently that people are gasping and I can hear the plane's metal creak. And outside the windows, on both sides of the plane, there are these incredible branching trees of lightning that would be really amazing to look at under completely different circumstances.

Now, I freely admit that *anytime* I'm on an airplane, I think I'm about to die. But on this flight, we *all* think we're about to die. It's actually sort of vindicating. A part of me wants to stand up, swirl my finger in the air, and say: *You see this? This is what I was afraid of all those other times, when you people were merrily munching your peanuts and reading your magazines!*

But I don't stand up and say those things, because both my arms are clutching the armrests and my legs are braced in a solid crash-landing V. The plane has stopped feeling like a flying living room and started feeling like the Kingdom Come Roller Coaster. At any moment, I expect the little oxygen things to drop. I don't know how better to describe it than to say it's exactly like living through the scene in a movie of what a plane does right before it crashes.

The guy behind me starts vomiting into a bag, and the woman across the aisle is having some sort of panic attack or asthma attack or something. I'm on the brink of a total meltdown, but doing everything

I can to hold it in, because I can't help thinking: *You know he's vomiting, and she's hyperventilating . . . if I just start sobbing, it really isn't going to be helpful.*

So, instead of crying, I find myself talking to God. This is odd, because I don't ordinarily talk to God—I'm not even sure I believe in God—but, hey, if ever there was a good time to start talking to an imaginary friend who lives in the sky, now'd be it.

As the plane shakes and plunges, I squeeze my eyes shut and focus my thoughts. *God, if you can hear me, I am so sorry for all the ways I've failed you, and I'm so grateful for all you've given me in this life. There's been a whole lot of shite, yes. But you've also given me far more joy than I deserve, and I know I don't say so very often, but I really appreciate it.*

Guess who isn't talking anymore? The pilot. The pilot's MIA, and I can only assume that either he's using both hands to try to regain control of his plane or he's on the horn with air traffic control, dictating his will. When he finally comes over the speaker again, he says: "We're in the middle of a lightning storm, but I'm going to get us through it." Then he adds: "Flight attendants, I need you to strap yourselves in."

I really didn't need to hear that last part. "I'm going to get us through this"—that's good. Why not stick with the happy, positive part? Then, if you need to give further instructions, you could just say: "Flight attendants, could you do that thing we discussed earlier?" Or you could get all military and give it a code name: "Flight attendants, I need you to Monkey-10." There's no need to alarm the civilians who are trying really hard not to sob by making us feel that something even *worse* than what we're already experiencing is about to happen.

We make it through the lightning storm, and when the plane lands safely, everyone bursts into hoots of applause, as if they've just seen the best Broadway show of their lives. A few people start to cry, because death could still be right around the corner, but at least it's death on the ground. I feel panicky and disoriented. My first thought is: *Oh my God*

I'm never getting on another plane for as long as I live. And my second thought is: *Oh my God my connecting flight takes off in twenty minutes.*

When my mother and father got married, in July 1967, they planned to honeymoon in Europe. They lived in Boston, and it took two flights to get overseas. The first flight, from Boston to New York, was so turbulent and terrifying for my mother that when they landed at JFK, she made perhaps the first serious request of her young marriage.

"Please don't make me get on another plane right now," she said. "I can't do it. I'm begging you. Please don't force me to go back up in the air."

In July 1967, my mother and father were madly in love. They were holding hands in an airport, wearing their chic, new honeymoon clothes. They had packed suitcases, booked hotels, bought travel guides, made reservations. My mother had blond hair that bent up at the neck, and she looked so much like Catherine Deneuve in *Belle de Jour* that when I first saw that movie, I almost couldn't watch. My father had dark-rimmed glasses and looked a bit like the husband on *Bewitched*. At that point in time, none of the other stuff had happened—she hadn't tried to run him over with the car or locked him in the basement or poured a bucket of water on his half of the bed. And he hadn't spat in her face or gritted his teeth when he spoke her name or begun carrying condoms in his briefcase. During a moment of rapprochement, when my father went to put on a condom, my mother hadn't asked: "Where'd you get that?" and when my father said, "My briefcase," she hadn't said, "Don't use those. I poked a pin through all of them."

In July 1967, my father was madly in love, and his comely new bride was begging him, with tears in her eyes, not to make her get on a plane again. So he didn't. They canceled the rest of the trip, spent the weekend in New York City, and used the leftover money to buy their living room furniture, which they forever after referred to as "the honeymoon divan" and "the honeymoon love seat."

If I want to bail on the second leg of my flight, there's historic precedent. There's genetic predisposition. After hearing my parents' honeymoon story countless times, for the first time in my life, I truly empathize with my mother's position. I really, *really* don't want to get on another plane. But standing there, like a stone amid the branching river of travelers, surrounded by airport bars and ATMs and newsstands in the middle of this hub airport that's in the middle of America, I feel I'm at a crossroads, as, indeed, I am. To some extent, our fate is predestined, but to some extent, we choose it.

I step forward and decide. I will get on that plane. I will not be my mother.

As I approach the gate, with every step I'm feeling kind of brave, and then, as soon as I cross that little crack of air that indicates I'm officially on another airplane, all pretense falls away, and I grab one of the flight attendants and say, in a clearly desperate voice: "I need to speak with the pilot." The flight attendant allows me into the cockpit, which seems kind of astonishing, considering I'm not sure I'm doing my best impression of a sane person at this moment.

In the cockpit, there are these two guys in hats, and I try to calm down and put a lid on my panic.

"Listen," I say, "I know you have your radar and your sonar and all your fancy equipment in here. But I want you to know there are *lightning bolts* up there."

I start out seminormal, but after a few seconds, I'm going on about how no one's careful anymore, everyone just wants to get where they're going in a hurry, the whole culture has become this reckless, intoxicated animal on a fast track to destruction. I tell them very urgently that if they see any lightning coming up, I want them to turn away, to please *turn away from the lightning*.

Then, for some reason—maybe it's PTSD—after I mention the lightning, I start to cry. It's as if all the tears I held back on the other plane are coming out on this one. These poor guys in their hats—they clearly have no idea what to do with me, and I'm well aware that I'm breaking rule number one of the Pilot Code of Manliness: *No weeping in the cockpit.*

But these guys surprise me. They are monumentally great. They stand up and shake my hand, and one says: "My name is Mike, and this is Chris, and we're going to be extremely careful. We promise. We want to get there safely just as much as you do. My wife just had a baby, and he has a two-month-old son at home, and we're both going to be really, really careful."

So, maybe it's okay if some pilots are allowed to talk some of the time.

As I make my way to my seat, one flight attendant offers me a cup of water and another one offers me a Xanax. It's not clear how they all simultaneously know there's a crazy person on board, and I'm it, but they do. I suspect that for *that* type of communication, they really do keep it under wraps. *Listen up, flight attendants. We've got a curlicue french fry in 29C. Curlicue fry in 29C.*

I take my seat in the twenty-ninth row and pull out my book. It's *The Best American Short Stories*, edited by Tobias Wolff. Too shaken up to read, I just hold it in my lap and look at it. Looking at it makes me happy. The orange cover is textured like papier-mâché, and when I turn on the overhead light, it almost seems to glow in my hands like a lantern.

Something about this book has been speaking to me. I was never really moved by the old-timey short stories they fed me in high school, but this book feels mysteriously familiar and true. It feels like the answer to a question I didn't know I'd asked.

My second flight of the day is uneventful—the pilots must have listened to me and turned away from the lightning—so much so that

I'm actually able to close my eyes for a while. Though exhausted, I'm too rattled to sleep, so I just slip in and out of the dreamy hypnagogic state in which past, present, and future meet.

Only when the plane lands safely in California, when the rubber wheels make contact with the runway and my torso bumps briefly against the seat, does it come to me. The question must have been dislodged during the turbulence and been rising through my consciousness, but it only emerges once I'm securely on the ground. As the lights blink on and a bell tone chimes and the other passengers gather their belongings, I remain in my seat, holding my book. *If I died tonight, would there be something I regretted, something else I'd wish I'd done with my brief time on earth?*

That winter, back in New York, I finally land a job. Maybe all the sangria my sister and I drank did cast some sort of spell, because it happens suddenly, unexpectedly. I take a writing class at the Sixty-Third Street Y from the wife of the copy chief of a business magazine. The teacher likes me, and it just so happens that the magazine needs a proofreader, so the copy chief calls me up. During the interview, I mention that I'm not a numbers person like my father, not in the least, just in case someone at the business magazine harbors a secret hope that I'm some sort of math genius. But the copy chief assures me the job is straight proofreading—very little math.

Unaccustomed to having to be somewhere at a specific time each day, I struggle a little with this at first. But the other people in my department don't seem to mind if I'm consistently twenty minutes late or my blouse is missing a button or my hair is flattened around my ears in the way hair might get flattened, say, by a sleep mask. The other people on the copy desk don't care about these things, because everyone on the copy desk is an artist in exile. There's an Icelandic poet, a folk guitarist, a hand model, a children's book author, an actress, a novelist, a short-story writer, and a playwright. They are witty, warm, and out of their minds. They are mine.

They soon become like family, which means the other people in my department can make fun of me, and I can make fun of them, but it's always in that friendly stab-you-with-love way that family members do. One day, my boss, who is also a novelist, compliments my haircut.

"Thanks," I say, beaming. "I cut it myself!"

"On just the one side?" he asks.

The job is wonderful. It's so much more than a job. It's a place where, finally, I can slow down and figure things out. No one scrutinizes me, so I don't have to perform. No one interrogates me, so I don't have to lie. It's a place where I can come out of my shell and walk around.

Plus, it bolsters my spirits to be earning an income. And I'm good at it. Proofreading comes naturally, because I'm a very slow reader with a healthy dose of OCD. In fact, it's as if proofreading were made for me. I call my sisters—at this point, one is in business school, another is in acting school, and the third is in college—and tell them that if they ever have a grammar emergency, I'm their girl. Everyone seems relieved, either because they know they'll never have to face down a verb tense alone again, or because it looks as if I might actually be pulling out of a tailspin.

Because of the job, I allow myself a dog. One Saturday afternoon, I go back to my old haunt, Pets on Lex, and find the loneliest puppy in the store. When I ask to hold her, she hides her face in my hair, and, after that, I just never put her down. She's a dappled miniature dachs-hund, and even when she weighs only 2.5 pounds and fits in my shoe, her personality is huge. She prances on the avenue as if each step were her way of announcing: "I'm here! I'm here!" and I wind up having to budget an extra twenty minutes to buy my morning coffee because so many people stop to admire her. More than once, a stranger gasps when he sees her coming and tells me: "That is the cutest dog I've ever seen."

But the day I rescue her from the pet store, she's still afraid. Even though I wrap her in my sweater, she can't stop trembling. With her swaddled in my arms, I hail a cab and scoot in the back seat, along with her crate, some treats, a bag of food, two bowls, and a squeaky armadillo. And just like that, I have a new best friend.

I'd like to say there's some epiphany, some big, dramatic moment like there is in the movies I love. I wish I could depict a climactic scene that drags me, spectacularly, into my proper place in life. But in reality, things just gradually, slowly, start to get better. When the day comes that I wake up and realize something has shifted, and it seems likely that I'm going to make it in the world after all, there's only one thing I want to do. I want to tell my father.

I get the idea to write him a letter and leave it on his grave, and I decide to do it on New Year's Eve, because that seems a fitting day to say goodbye to the past and mark a new beginning. I rent a car, but I haven't visited his grave since the funeral—it could be that I've felt ashamed—and I was so dazed with grief when my family buried him that I didn't pay any attention to where the cemetery was. My father lived in New Canaan, Connecticut, so I assume he's buried in the New Canaan cemetery. But when I get there, it's dark and cold and nothing looks familiar.

Nothing looks familiar because I not only have the wrong cemetery, I have the wrong state. By the time I find a phone, call my uncle, figure out he's buried in Banksville, New York, and drive there, it's approaching midnight.

Even when I make it to the right town, I still can't find the cemetery, which is troubling, because the level of incompetence I'm displaying in locating my own father's grave is undercutting my conviction that I'm going to be okay, the celebration of which was the whole point of this trip in the first place. Nevertheless, I keep my chin up, and flag down a passing motorist.

"Do you know how to get to the Middle Patent Rural Cemetery?"

The guy in the car seems off, as if he's out trolling for trouble, and he avoids eye contact.

"The really old one?" he says, staring straight ahead. "Where the Revolutionary War soldiers are buried?"

"That's the one."

He knows where it is and tells me, but I get a chill as he drives away, as if maybe it wasn't my sharpest move ever to let a creepy-looking guy, alone in his car at midnight, know I'm on my way to a cemetery by myself. But, by the time this thought occurs to me, there's nothing to be done.

The cemetery is beautiful, cloaked in moonlight. There's so much I didn't take in the day my father was buried. There's an antique water pump at the base of a hill, a stone angel pointing fiercely into the distance, and a stand of elegant, stately trees. A fat moon rests just above the silhouetted treetops, bright as a spotlight.

I locate my father's plot and kneel beside it in the snow. He never had much interest in religion; there's no cross or line from scripture on his grave. When he was dying, his friends joked that he should be cremated and have his ashes scattered over the New York Stock Exchange. The bare stone spells out a single word: BLACK.

Wispy flakes of snow have begun to fall, but it isn't cold. When I touch it, his headstone feels warmer than the air. I keep my palm pressed against it for a long moment.

When it comes time to leave him the letter, I imagine that my father is listening and can hear me. I try to believe that he lives—as I so often strongly feel—on just the other side of an invisible veil.

"Everything you did for me, everything you taught me—it wasn't wasted," I manage to say. "I know it didn't look very promising for a while there, but I found a place in the world."

I start to cry then, because it seems so impossible, and yet I did—I found a place.

A soft loneliness clings to the air like frost. I close my eyes, remembering his final words. "You didn't let me down—you could never let me down. You pointed the way," I say. "I got a dog—" The thought of the dog makes me cry again. "She's a willful rascal. The two of you would have loved each other."

I lift the letter to my lips, kiss it, and nestle it in the snow, leaning it against his headstone. I leave one of the mechanical pencils he used to love so much beside it, as a gift.

Even though I don't want to leave, I know it's time to go, time to tell him what I've traveled years and miles to say.

"You don't have to worry about me anymore," I whisper.

And the instant I say the word "anymore," I see the rippling flash of moonlight against a man's shirt.

My energy exits through my feet, and as I stand there, paralyzed, I suddenly realize that there were moments in my life before this when I believed I was experiencing fear, but I was wrong. *This* is fear. Mixed in with a nauseating vertigo and the dizzying premonition of my own death, I find something else, something that surprises me.

I am incredulous.

Wow, I think. *I wouldn't have believed someone would actually have the audacity to come and kill me at my father's grave, but I guess I was wrong. Well—live and learn.*

I try to be someone who looks fate in the eye, but not on this night. After the initial sighting, I keep my gaze lowered—I don't want to see the ax, or the rope, or the gun. I don't want to see the eyes that were previously so shy now taking me in with eager hunger.

A minute passes. Then another. The cemetery is quiet; only the wind stirs. From the woods, I sense the watchful presence of solemn deer.

By the time I lift my head and discover it's not a man's shirt, but an American flag that's rippling in the moonlight, it's as if some invisible part of me has already broken loose and flown away, slipping down through all the graves, past bone and rock and water, way down deep to the ululating center of the earth.

For the rest of my life, when I think of this night, its edges will remain scalloped in mystery. I will wonder if I didn't somehow find for myself the exact kind of rite-of-passage moment I must have subconsciously been seeking. I will wonder what became of the letter—which was gone on subsequent visits—and presume it was swept up and thrown away by the groundskeeper. I will wonder about the

Revolutionary War soldiers buried there—if any of their descendants ever visited, laying flowers upon earth their forebears had won. And I'll wonder about the angel, with her fierce eyes and one arm extended, as if trying to draw my attention to some vista of the unseen realms.

JESUS

I've become a believer. I don't understand how it happened. I was read-ing a book, and when I started the book, I did not believe in Jesus Christ, but when I finished it, I did.

I find this sudden belief in Jesus very odd, as does everyone else in my life—even the word *Jesus* feels uncomfortable to me—but I'm will-ing to roll with it. Life's a mystery; strange things happen. What strikes me as most odd is how involuntary my conversion was. I was sitting in a blue corduroy chair on an ordinary Tuesday afternoon, book in hand, when faith seemed to overtake me like water. Because it did not feel like a choice, I still feel deeply connected to the world of nonbelievers—I was one myself, for so long—and I insist that a God who makes his sun to shine on the just as well as the unjust can also make his heaven a reward for everyone. This is, in fact, my lifelong prayer.

On Friday, August 13, 1999, I'm sitting in my living room, feeling bad for Satan, when something peculiar happens. Because I've come to reli-gion as an adult, I've brought with me a boatload of highly reasonable questions. All week, I've been reading about God's boundless mercy, and I find myself dwelling on it, this hot August afternoon, as I sip my ginger tea in the comfort of my living room. I'm feeling in awe of the idea that no human being can ever fall so low that God won't welcome him back immediately, with open arms, if only he repents. And I can't help wondering if this same principle applies to the angels, since I know that devils are just angels who, like man, fell. In short, I've been wondering if Lucifer and his pals could ever turn themselves in, and be forgiven. Even though I don't know the answer, I have a sinking feeling that, for some reason, the boundlessness of God's mercy excludes them—although, if it does, it would not be boundless—which makes me feel bad. And it's in this moment that a snake appears.

Yes, a snake. Yes, I'd been thinking about Satan. And, yes, it was Friday the thirteenth.

Now, right off the bat—before I even move to defend myself—I'd like to mention that this is something I would never, *ever*, put in a piece of fiction. This is a triple no-no, this snake/Satan/thirteen thing. It's beyond awful, and it's just begging people to hate me and throw my book out the window. I would never do that, or anything remotely like that, in one of my stories.

But, apparently, God can do whatever he likes in his.

Up until the snake appeared, I'd been feeling bad, but I also felt buoyant, because I love lazy afternoons like this, where I'm able to spend hours on end just thinking and reading in the gentle quiet of my home. Not only has my magazine job given me a sense of community and a steady income, but, after a couple of years, I feel rooted enough that I find I want to buy a house. This is my first house—I moved here, to Dutchess County, from Manhattan six months ago—and I've been relishing the solitude of country life. On the days of the week that I have to be at my desk in Midtown, I ride the Saw Mill River Parkway with the radio on and let the light pour in through the sunroof. On weekends, if I've had my fill of solitude, there's a club where they play live music just down the road, called the Towne Crier. The house is a stone-faced cottage that was built in 1952 and used to be a summer getaway for city dwellers. From the first moment I saw it, I was in love—it has a wood-burning stove, a wraparound deck, and panoramic views of Whaley Lake. It's just perfect. Except for the snake.

At first, I don't realize it's a snake. I'm sitting in my blue corduroy chair—the same chair in which faith overtook me just a few weeks ago—and I look up from my book because my dog has started barking furiously at the baseboard heater. But when I look where she's obviously urging me to look, all I see is a band of moving colors in the gap between the heater and the carpet; my eyes fail to register it as a snake. This is because I'm an idiot, yes, but it's also because I'm just not used to seeing snakes.

Once my mind focuses and I realize it's a snake—a moving snake— I also realize that this is very, very bad, because at any moment, I could lose track of the snake inside my house and not know where he's hiding, which would mean, obviously, that I'd have to move. So I jump up from my chair, both acutely aware that I must stop the snake and acutely unaware of how to do so. I stand in place. The snake is still moving. The dog is barking even more ferociously. My hands are sweating, and my heart is fluttering, but my mind is blank. Then, without thinking, I step toward the baseboard heater and say in a very firm voice:

"Stop, Snakie!"

And Snakie stops.

Now, I know perfectly well that Snakie cannot understand what I've said. But the vibrations of my voice or the heat of my body must have reached him, because he's motionless. There he is—this shocking, surprisingly long creature, easily as long as my arm span, with his elaborate beige-, brown-, and black-patterned skin.

The dog is apoplectic; she obviously wants a piece of him. But I know without a doubt who'd win that showdown—I can envision a bulge the size and shape of a ten-pound miniature dachshund inside the snake. I scoop her up and lock her in the back bedroom.

Then I try my best to figure out how to get rid of this thing. With my eyes constantly surveilling him, I call the pest-control people, who were at my house earlier in the day to lay mousetraps. Now they tell me—rather joyfully, it seems—that they don't handle snakes. Next I call the sheriff, who lives just down the road, but he informs me—also with notable enthusiasm—that local government is not responsible for snake removal. Finally, I call the DEC, the Department of Environmental Conservation.

A nice lady answers on the first ring. "Hello, DEC."

"There's a snake in my living room."

"Well, they sure as heck don't call it Friday the thirteenth for nothing!" she says without missing a beat, and, for the third time, I note a disconcerting amount of excitement in the voice on the other end of the line.

And, sure enough, even though she's ready with her snappy riposte, it turns out the nice lady from the DEC can't help me, either.

I'm at a loss. I could call my neighbors, who wear overalls and seem like they might know what to do about a snake, but I don't know their number. I could run outside and knock on their door, but then I'd risk losing track of the snake, and I don't want to move yet; I love this house. I have no choice. I'm going to have to wrangle this beast myself.

It's clear to me, even now, that this decision does not indicate bravery. In fact, it's bravery's opposite—it's fear, mixed with a healthy dollop of stupidity. I'm so afraid of the snake that I'm going to have to wrangle it; otherwise I might lose track of the snake, and then the snake wins.

And, as all this is happening, I can't help thinking about the symbolic implications. I am, admittedly, a person who sometimes reads into things. When I hear a Steve Winwood song on the radio, I know I'm about to get good news. When I see a cardinal, I know my grandmother is near. When I break off the big half of a wishbone—even if I also break off the little half, because I'm breaking it with myself—I know the first wish I make will come true. Yet somehow, when I'm knee-deep in what is arguably the most symbolically charged episode of my life, I fail to see any veiled meaning. Symbolism is a luxury only afforded in retrospect.

When an idea finally hits me, I leave the snake alone just long enough to race to the kitchen, fetch a big bucket I keep under the sink, grab the newspaper, and race back. Then I very slowly approach the snake with my bucket and my paper, trying to telegraph the idea that I'm a nice person. I think benign thoughts. I keep my breathing relaxed. The snake, however, does not get the message. As soon as I'm within three feet of him, he rears up and flicks his tongue out at me.

My jaw drops. This is something I thought only cartoon snakes did; in real life, I thought they just slithered around on the ground.

The snake's tongue has gone back in, but his head remains reared. I take a step back. I want no part of that. From the bedroom, the dog, sensitive to proximate animal drama, is barking herself silly, and I tele-pathically tell her to shut her trap because I'm worried she's annoying Snakie. My plan *had* been to use the newspaper to gently escort the snake into the bucket, where he could coil up like a living water hose. Then I'd clamp the newspaper over him, carry him outside, and dump him in the woods. But, apparently, my plan isn't going to work.

This should probably be the part where I start praying for Jesus and his holy hosts of angels to stop playing poker and help me out already, but no. I don't pray. I'm still new to religion at this point, and it doesn't come naturally to ask for help.

For a while, there's a standoff. I watch Snakie; Snakie watches me. He doesn't try to tempt me into eating anything, and I don't try to crush his head with my heel. If he begins to move deeper into the house, I intend to start screaming, stomping, and spitting at him. If he moves toward me, I'll run. Yes, my options are the same ones a five-year-old might come up with. But I can't think of anything better.

The afternoon light slants in sideways. The house is perfectly still. After a while, I sit in my chair again, because a standoff is weary business, and my back is starting to hurt. The snake isn't going anywhere, and neither am I. I have all the time in the world to wait him out. The way I see it, some sort of solution will eventually present itself. Some sort of solution always does.

The dog is still barking, the sun is still setting, the snake is still in my living room. I've been brainstorming for over an hour, and I've been so focused on trying to come up with an ingenious snake-wrangling solution that I've failed to see the simple one staring me in the face. To get Snakie to leave my house, all I have to do is open the front door. The animal immediately senses the warm air, feels the breeze from the woods, and slithers out.

But, before he's disappeared from sight, I grab my camera and snap a quick photo—not so I can brag about my Saint Patrick exploits, but so I can look up what kind of snake he is and determine if he's poisonous, because, if he is, I still might have to move.

THE SQUATTY
KILLERS

The plan is to go to my grandmother's old, abandoned house for a week, so I can finish writing a book. Or a story. Or a paragraph. Really, I'd just like to finish *something*. Ever since I had an epiphany about my life after a harrowing plane ride, I've been trying to write, but the distractions of the world keep intervening. So, with my house free of serpents and a week off from work, I figure I'll go somewhere where my distractions can't find me.

My grandmother on my mother's side has a two-story ranch at the end of a sleepy cul-de-sac in Arlington, Massachusetts. She has Alzheimer's and lives with my uncle now, so she won't be there, unfortunately. As a young girl, she was what people referred to as "black Irish"—dark haired, with a pale complexion—and she was always skinny, despite claiming she had the appetite of twelve men. Her father died in the Spanish flu pandemic when she was only two years old, and her mother, Alice, who had five children—four boys and then my nana—owned a celery farm. Nana is tough and kind and always upbeat; to be honest, I don't know where she gets her energy. I'm hoping that being in her psychic space might have a positive influence on my writing. When I told her about my airplane epiphany, she, too, confided that she'd always wanted to be a writer. In the 1930s, she even penned a story that won some sort of high school competition. She can remember the opening line, *Dear Sergeant Knowles and all your companions*, but she can't remember anything after that, nor what might have been exceptional about it. Maybe it's that she was writing in the male voice? Or addressing dead people? I tell her it's a good opening line and that I'll try to get in touch with the Arlington High School archivist and see if I can hunt down the story for her, but I never do.

It takes about four hours to get to my grandmother's, and I could have left at any point in the afternoon, and I probably would have, if I were a normal person. But I'm me, so I don't leave until ten at night, which means I arrive at my nana's house at two in the morning.

As soon as I get there, I can tell something isn't right. The screen is hanging at a sharp angle, and the front door is unlocked. These are disturbing discoveries, but the human brain is a wonderful rationalization machine, so I think, *Oh. The wind must have blown the screen off its hinges. And the last person to leave must have forgotten to turn the lock. No big deal.*

So I open the door and step inside, and as I do, I hear a sound—an incredibly loud, alarming sound—although at first I can't identify what it is. I cautiously follow the sound to my nana's bedroom at the back of the house, and when I enter the room, there's an old TV set playing static at a volume so loud as to be incomprehensible. It's as if the antique device has abnormal settings that were made for, say, interplanetary travel, in case someone wanted to still be able to hear his TV from outer space. I might have thought this white-noise-screaming television was as disturbing as the unlocked front door, if I had a chance to think. But all my mental energy is being consumed with trying to turn the damn thing off. Because it won't turn off. I switch the knob back and forth and forth and back, but it stays on, no matter how many times I switch it.

Okay, no problem, says my brain. *Obviously, a lightning bolt struck the power grid, and the TV turned on through some other special way—it could happen—and I need to find some other special way to turn it off.* Ultimately, unplugging it works.

My next order of business is to use the bathroom, because I've been on the road for four hours. But when I go in the bathroom—which has powder-pink fixtures and a plantless planter full of old coins I used to play with as a kid—there's no water in the toilet. In fact, not only is there no water in the toilet, but at the very bottom of the bowl, where the water should be, there's blood.

Okay, no problem, says my brain. *Obviously, an animal of some sort got into the plumbing and died in there. So . . . I'll just use the bathroom downstairs.* But when I get to the downstairs toilet, there's blood in that one, too.

Now, at this point, do I decide there must be cultish squatters who've been performing religious sacrifices inside my grandmother's old, abandoned house? Or that maybe a crazy neighbor has chopped up his wife and tried to destroy the evidence? No. Not consciously, anyway. What I consciously think is, *Oh, right. Well, if an animal died in the plumbing, it would obviously contaminate both toilets—duh.*

So I proceed as if nothing were wrong. I bring in my bags, put on my pj's, brush my teeth, and crawl into bed. I basically do everything that anyone who's ever watched a horror movie knows I'm expected to do.

Safely nestled between my grandmother's sheets, beneath a webbed slipcover that reminds me of a doily, I try to sleep. Tomorrow is going to be a big day. Tomorrow, I might finish something—it could happen. The house feels creepy, yes. But maybe it's fitting that I should attempt to write in a place that feels spooky, because writing itself feels spooky to me.

On the nightstand, I've stacked a pile of books. When I'm not writing, I plan to read. Ever since the airplane, this has been my strategy for my homeschool MFA: read, write, throw away. Something inside me believes that I can learn how to write on my own. I can already feel it happening.

For some strange reason having nothing to do with the poltergeist TV or the bloody toilets, I can't sleep. I just lie there, nice and still, so as not to disturb any evil spirits. This goes on for a while, until the moment arrives when I reach for the nightstand and my hand lands on the longest, sharpest pair of scissors I've ever seen. As in, I didn't know they made scissors this long and scary except as props in Tod Browning movies.

And this is when I actually begin to panic. Because, obviously, the last person in the house—before she'd been, you know, murdered and stuffed in the toilet—had felt exactly the same way I'm feeling now. She had *known* she was in danger, and she had placed this very pair of scissors right here next to the pillow, where they'd be within easy reach when her killer approached. If only she'd grabbed them in time.

I feel my own pulse throbbing in my neck, and it dawns on me that maybe now is when I should attempt to pray the rosary or something. I don't know how to pray the rosary; I've never even held a pair of rosary beads. My grandmother, however, is a devout Irish Catholic who goes to Mass daily, prays the rosary nightly, and speaks of "God's plan" with the same nonchalance with which most people speak of Dunkin' Donuts. I'm sure there must be at least a dozen strands of rosary beads strewn about this house, and if I could just get my hands on one of them, maybe my mouth would start forming the words on its own, the way it might in a slasher flick, since that's obviously what I'm living. I'd like to look for said rosary beads, but by this point, I'm pretty sure the killers or the squatters or whatever they are—the squatty killers—are somewhere in the house with me.

Fear has me chained to my grandmother's bed, where all that's left to do is await my own death. To arrest my mounting panic, I hit the pause button. I think of my life as a story. I consider the plot. This would make a terrible plot. After all I've been through, to be murdered in my grandmother's old, abandoned house by a cultish squatter with a pair of scissors? I am rejecting this plot on its literary merits. Not to mention that to be murdered in this house that still smells of my nana, that still has that cinnamon-nutmeg–Special K smell, would be so wrong.

Alone in her room, surrounded by all her knickknacks, my thoughts turn to my nana. I can see her clearly in my mind's eye: white hair brighter than milk, the gap between her two front teeth that breaks open when she smiles. She lived through the Great Depression and two world wars, yet I have never once seen her truly afraid. I have lived an extremely easy life by comparison, yet I am truly afraid about once a week.

If she were here, there'd be no room for fear. Even as her mind degrades and her strength grows dim, she seems steadfast. The truth is I'm more afraid of her death than she is.

"What'll I do when I don't have you anymore?" I asked the last time I saw her.

Her gaze transmitted its usual brilliance. "You'll always have me," she said.

It's four in the morning when I hear something crunching in the backyard. I bolt upright in bed and, listening acutely, hear it again: the unmistakable sound of footsteps. *No,* I tell myself, *no, no, no, it can't be*—and then, when the noise draws closer, I finally lose it. I jump out of bed, grab my phone, and frantically call my uncle. "Uncle Carl!" I say. "The TV wouldn't stop playing static and there's blood in all the toilets and a killer in the backyard! Call me!" Because of course I'm leaving a message. Because my uncle goes to bed at nine thirty.

I'm not exactly sure how I make it through the night—I have no memory of actually sleeping—but when my uncle calls back in the morning,

I'm squatting on the southwest corner of the bed, facing the backyard, gripping the scissors. This, apparently, is what I felt to be my best defensive position.

My uncle's voice is coming through the phone receiver. "What?" I say hoarsely, my brain only dimly awake, and he begins to explain that he put the TV on a timer, to keep thieves away—which of course makes sense, because crooks are afraid of TVs—and he drained both toilets and filled them with antifreeze, and the noise in the backyard is the neighborhood woodchuck, who likes to forage for food in the wee hours.

While he's speaking, my body floods with relief, I realize how desperately I need sleep, and my eyes slowly come into focus. There's a female cardinal perched on a branch in the backyard. My nana loves cardinals. The bird sits primly, and, as another second of time slips by, I stop listening to whatever my uncle is saying as a cold bolt zips from my scalp to my tailbone. The cardinal—it's unmistakable—she's staring straight at me, and for a split second I'd swear it's not the cardinal who holds me in her gaze. It's my grandmother.

I stick out the rest of the week in my nana's old house, and while I don't actually finish anything, I make progress, which is something. During the day, I eat Italian subs from D'Agostino's while I dream up sentences on a park bench as the slow trains rumble through Winchester Center. At night, I read from one of my books until my thoughts grow bleary and my eyes close. After I switch off the light, I always grope around on the nightstand to make sure the scissors are still there at the ready, just in case.

My grandmother lives for a few more years after this, until she dies at the age of ninety-six while staying at my uncle's house in Virginia. She passes away one crisp March day when the cherry trees have already turned to bud, and her church friends say she's on her way to see her father again. My life carries on, and, except for certain special days, I don't often think of her. But her old gray house still sits there, empty, and even though I eventually move far away, to another coast, some starless nights I can still feel it waiting there at the end of the cul-de-sac, whispering to the circling winds, pulling from its endless cache of stories.

DATING GAMES

I have a theory about time. That it's a trickster, a mirage. That when matter becomes light—as it does when it moves fast enough—time collapses, and that there's light—timelessness—inside us all.

I'd like someone to discuss my theories with, so I run a personal ad in *New York* magazine. In the little thumbnail paragraphs, I request "a young Glenn Gould / Richard Feynman" type. This seems perfectly reasonable. I don't lead with Feynman, though; my first line is: *Blond, blue-eyed Harvard graduate, 29, seeks kind and brilliant man who is intellectually uninhibited, socially independent, and spiritually intrigued.* After that, in addition to referencing Feynman and Gould, I attempt to describe my simultaneous desires for companionship and solitude.

This does not lead to romance. One person openly admits: *I'm not at all what you're looking for, but I really liked your ad!* Other responders are perhaps not as self-aware. I receive a memorable offer from someone who wants to set me up with his friend who is "slightly schizophrenic" but also a bona fide genius. There is no Goldilocks ending, and I journey into my thirties not wanting to be lonely but often wanting to be alone. Yet even as I crave it, I have a hard time describing what it is about solitude that I find so compelling. It's partly that it's so spiritually and creatively rich. But it could also be that my formative years—all of us under one roof, with so much crazy fighting—were more traumatic than I realize. Perhaps it's only when I'm alone that I feel completely safe.

For months, my mother has been scouring furniture stores in a quest to find a coffee table to go in front of an ocean-view window in her Florida condo. She brings it up on almost every phone call, and whenever I visit, its absence is glaring. She claims she's searching for something stunning but invisible, which makes me laugh, until I realize that a stunning but invisible man might be just what I need.

I date. My success at dating could best be described as mixed. It's difficult to parse what I mean when I say I want to be with someone but I also want to be alone. Also, it seems that as soon as I describe myself as a free spirit who's not really interested in marriage, some men decide I'm the exact one they should marry.

At times, dating exemplifies all the ways in which I don't understand the dynamics of the human mind. "I despise eggplant," I tell a handsome, witty editor, on our first date.

"Oh, I could make you some eggplant that you'd like," he says. In response, I only smile. I don't say: *Yes, but why would you make me eggplant when there are five thousand vegetables and I've just told you it's the* one *vegetable I hate?*

There's a performative aspect to nonsolitude that comes naturally to me—I'm high empathy, and I can sense how to please—but it's draining. It's only when I'm alone that I feel most relaxed, most myself.

Still, love creeps in. It creeps in like the violet weed that blankets the highway embankments with blossoms each spring. There are all kinds of ways to meet a kindred spirit—to encounter a like mind—and more than once, I sit in my blue corduroy chair, press an open book to my chest, and weep.

I meet the Last of the Last Great Men after reading his work. I connect with his two short-story collections so deeply that by the time

I finish the final story, it's as if I've had a religious experience. The first time I ask if he'd like to get coffee, he says he's busy grading papers. The second time, he has a dentist appointment. But the third time I ask, his papers are graded and his teeth are clean.

We meet at the Half King for a drink. He's seventeen years my senior, but his appearance and demeanor are youthful. He actually looks *better* than his author photo—a rare occurrence—which was taken in the days before he wore a goatee. There's something appealingly self-contained about him, as if he isn't really looking for anything; he's just motoring along, doing his work. I never play games with people—*why should I pretend to be coy or mysterious, when I'm so genuinely independent?*—and we hit it off right away.

"Shall we order another drink?"

"Absolutely!"

"Hungry for some appetizers?"

"Indeed!"

"How about we go for dinner at La Lunchonette?"

He moves in three weeks later. I worry that the transition from Greenwich Village to rural Dutchess County will be too jarring, but he writes on the back deck and plants tulips on the front lawn. Like me, he's not excessively kinetic—both of us basically like to read, write, and watch movies—plus he loves to cook, which is great, because I'm such a notoriously bad cook that the one time I tried to boil rice, I had to throw the pan away. Of course he's into jazz, which is probably my least favorite type of music, because somehow I only attract jazz-loving men. I pretend to be a jazz-loving woman until he figures me out and starts to play folk music during dinner instead. I wake one morning to find moonflower vines twining the posts that overlook the lake.

Somehow—bizarrely, cosmically—I have met my match.

PART III

CALIFORNIA SKY

You live thirty miles east of LA, in a town that's briefly mentioned in *Bill and Ted's Excellent Adventure*, so when you tell people where you live, they often start quoting Keanu Reeves lines or acting out scenes, which was a little weird at first, but now you're used to it.

You moved here six months ago, looking for a fresh start after a harrowing illness. You fell in love with California immediately. It wasn't just the weather and the ocean and the palm trees; it was something else—the vibrational frequency of the earth above these particular tectonic plates. You didn't used to believe in "vibrations," but ever since you got sick, you can actually feel them—which has given you a fresh perspective on all those Beach Boys songs. Some days you worry that the vibrations are simply a function of your proximity to the San Andreas Fault, true. But, still. All the sunshine in your new town puts you in a better mood. You lost everything you had—except your voice—during your mystery illness, so anything mood elevating is welcome. The best part about living here is it feels as if you've finally landed in the place where you were always meant to be. At the end of your cross-country drive, as soon as you hit the LA freeways, you looked around and said: "You know what this place needs? One more car."

It's Saturday afternoon, and you're sitting by the pool with your laptop, living the dream. Another family from your apartment building is here, living their dream, only their dream is quite a bit noisier than yours. Three little kids are splashing, screeching, and screaming the same way they might if they were being, say, flayed alive. You keep looking up from your work to see if one of them is, in fact, being flayed or water boarded or tortured in some way and needs your help, but no—they're just playing. You wonder, briefly, if it'd be possible to suggest to them in a non-obnoxious way that, perhaps, they could reserve the truly piercing screams for the most climactic moments in their playtime, as they'd have much more dramatic impact that way. To use the screams indiscriminately, as they are doing now, only robs them of their power. You could tell them this, but you don't, because if you did, you'd have to admit something to yourself: you are old.

At fortysomething, you realize that you're not old, technically, but you're older than you once were.

Because of your age, and because you're single and childless, a friend has recently suggested that you "freeze some eggs," as a way to keep your options open.

Even after you explain to your friend that you don't want a baby, she doesn't quite get it. Mystifyingly, she seems not to believe you. She says babies are like caviar—obviously disgusting until you actually eat it. Unless you try it, you'll never know. You tell her you have zero desire to eat a baby. "But are you sure?" she asks. "Are you really, really sure?"

You're sure, but you agree to babysit her six-month-old for a weekend, just to be certain.

No one advertises what the hours are for this job called motherhood, but you can report that the hours are terrible. You don't usually like to drink before noon, but the first day, after only six hours alone with the screaming baby, come lunchtime you find yourself eyeing the Sancerre in the fridge. You pour yourself a little glass, which you sip for a while, until the baby hurls a rubber giraffe at it with astonishing precision. He's locked in his seat, which is good, because it means you can clean up the spilled wine without him falling out and splitting his head open like a melon. He seems to enjoy the fact that you're down on your hands and knees, cleaning up his mess as if you were his little servant—which, actually, you are—and he takes this opportunity to launch more food at your hair. Food launching delights him, and suddenly he's happier than he's been all morning.

Sitting on the floor, you're unsure what the appropriate response to this is. Are you supposed to laugh it off, so everyone can keep having a good time, or scold him so he learns he's not supposed to throw food at people? The solution is unclear. This is one of the obvious pitfalls of motherhood: the unclearness of everything. In the end, you opt for a combination of the two, where, for a little while, you spin your eyeballs up as if you can see the Cheerios landing in your hair, and you think it's hilarious, then, when you slice your finger on a piece of broken glass, you get right up in the baby's face and say: "No! No throw food at Mommy!" in a voice so powerful it actually frightens both you and the baby. Without even trying, you manage to give him the most confusing, irrational, and emotionally damaging response of them all.

When it comes time to read the baby a story, you preview your options. Nothing looks good. *Baby Sees Spots and Dots*? You're surprised at the gobbledygook they've been feeding his developing brain. No wonder he throws his food! You decide to give him a taste of John Keats, to expand his horizons. Keats is what you were listening to during your drive up the coast.

You pull up *Endymion* on your phone and dig in, though not right at the beginning, because *Endymion* is long, and you want to get to the good part, the part that starts: "Life's self is nourished by its proper pith / And we are nurtured like a pelican brood," because that's the part you think the baby will like. And he does like it; the baby gurgles and coos, which makes you happy, so you drink some more wine, until soon you feel inspired to really act it out for him, because Keats sounds so much better when you commit to it with your whole body, so, before long, you're finishing off the rest of the wine and performing a little Keatsian parlor play for the baby, using his armada of stuffed animals as various character actors, including a spaceshiplike thing that has a string and makes noise and is not a character, exactly, but adds to the general excitement.

Afterward, you and the baby are both very tired, so you put him down for a nap in his crib, and, while doing so, you think you might like to lie down in the crib, too—it looks really comfy in there, and you haven't been inside a crib for quite some time, plus there's plenty of room. So you cozy on down with the baby for a nap. This turns out to be a great decision because, later, when you tell the baby's mum who was pestering you about freezing your eggs how you were drinking wine and reading Keats and taking a nap with her baby, she finally stops pestering you about freezing your eggs.

On the way home from your adventure in babysitting, as you ride the freeway from Berkeley back to LA, the sky is alive with one of the most ferocious sunsets you've ever seen. Once, when you were

THE QUIET MIRACLE OF A NORMAL LIFE

It's a simple scene: rural New York, late afternoon, early June. The sliding door to the back deck is open, and a light breeze from the lake skitters through the house like a spirit. Two overturned kayaks are resting out in the yard, and I'm resting, too. I prop my feet on the coffee table and examine my calf muscles. A fleeting thought comes to mind containing the phrase *get more exercise*—and it prompts me to hop up for a bottle of wine from the fridge. I'm still wearing the black bikini and cut-off shorts I wore when we went kayaking to the island. The Last of the Last Great Men snapped a selfie of the two of us that almost made us capsize.

The sauvignon blanc is in an elegantly tapered bottle the color of green sea glass. I like its cool heft in my hands, the snap of the cap as I twist it off.

I can see him out on the deck with his flip-flops and his tongs. When it was still winter, he sometimes used to wear the chef's toque I gave him for Christmas when he grilled, but today he's in a baseball cap. As I slide open the screen door, it makes a sound that evokes this particular summer, as well as every summer before: throwing tennis balls against the garage and learning to balance on a Bongo Board and my bare feet thudding against a wooden dock on Lake Winnipesaukee and waterskiing and crackling bonfires and my first kiss. I hand my boyfriend the glass of wine, kiss his cheek, and walk away without saying a word.

Inside the house, I carry my glass over to the bookshelf and study the titles, my free hand propped under my elbow.

I use my fingertip to pluck a slim volume by Tony Hoagland from the shelf and walk it to the bedroom to place it on the nightstand, for later. I'm only half aware of a feeling that hums in the soles of my feet as I do, something clear and simple but wide and beautiful, too. I am happy.

MAP TO AN UNKNOWN ILLNESS

I wake up in a sweat, with a fatigue that reaches to my marrow. Not only is the bed drenched in sweat, but it feels as if I've been run over by a truck in my sleep. It's the kind of feeling that makes me fear I'm dying, so I wait a few weeks before I go to the doctor. When he runs a battery of tests and declares me to be in perfect health, I blink at him in wonderment. I explain again: everything hurts, I have zero energy, on some mornings, when I first wake up, I can't see. The doctor shrugs and sends me home. When I get home, I crawl into bed and sleep for sixteen hours.

I'm healthy. I eat right. I occasionally kayak. I had my tonsils removed in 1992 and my mercury fillings replaced a few years ago with nontoxic substitutes when I discovered, one day, that I couldn't feel the left side of my face. This was a few months before my first book was scheduled to come out, so everyone told me it was "just nerves."

When I called my mother, she asked if I was having a stroke.

"A what?" I said, my blood pressure rising.

"A stroke!" she said. I was in the car while we were having this conversation, and, as she talked, I turned around and headed for the hospital.

~

After examining me, and a strange reticular rash on my leg, the doctors conferred, said it was probably some sort of virus, and sent me home.

A few weeks later, I developed digestive problems, and, through research and a few serendipities, I figured out that I was being poisoned by my teeth. Why are dentists still filling caries with a substance that's known to damage the nervous system when there are safer (if more expensive) options? I don't know; you'd have to take that up with the American Dental Association. The hunks of mercury in my mouth were not only more than thirty years old, they also degraded every time I ate or drank.

When I finally had my hair, urine, and blood tested for mercury, I had more than three times the average amount the CDC has found to exist across the population.

But aside from that notable experience, I've had very few encounters with doctors. The most time I've spent with medical professionals was during the weeks I stayed with my father after his cancer diagnosis, and that feels so long ago, almost another lifetime. In fact, it was exactly two decades ago, and I was a different person then—not only in the sense that the thirty-seven trillion cells of my body have been replaced, but in that my blueprint itself has somehow changed. When I see photographs of myself from that era, I'm tempted to ask the blond waif in red lipstick: *Who are you?*

A week after my first doctor visit, I go to a different doctor, to show her my furry brown tongue. She also runs a bunch of tests, also says I'm fine. Dumbfounded, I reiterate the part about my liver—how I have a dull, constant ache where my liver should be. With one hand, she holds up an ultrasound slide and says, "You've got a terrific liver! Enjoy it!" I stick out my tongue, not to be rude, but to display its disturbing appearance. "Some people just have brown, furry tongues!" she says. I ponder all the people I've known in my forty years, all the tongues. Not one of them resembled the beer-stained carpet at a fraternity house.

The doctor standing before me in her white coat appears perfectly sincere. I'm at one of the finest hospitals in the country, and it feels like April Fools' Day. When she tells me again that I'm the image of good health, I do not scream, *Are you honestly out of your mind?* Not only do I not say what I think, I don't say anything. Not because I believe her, but because I suffer from an absurd compulsion to be nice. Her framed diplomas, her mahogany desk, her shockingly white teeth: they all implore me to take her good news and run with it. But my body tells a different story.

At home, in the bathroom mirror, I scrutinize my face. My hair is falling out. It clogs the shower drain and hangs limply in an anemic ponytail. There are purple circles under my eyes. My fingernails are soft as wax. My skin, once dewy, has turned brittle overnight. I tell myself that now I have just enough wrinkles for people to take me seriously. But underneath the lie, my stomach twists. *What's going on?* Even the dog sniffs at me as if my scent has turned suddenly foreign. I'm still able to work—I do freelance copyediting, and my boyfriend does freelance web design—but I'm taking on fewer and fewer projects.

By the time I go to the third doctor, I've started forgetting things. I carry a list of symptoms in my purse. Sunlight—nearly all light—hurts my eyes. All sounds are too loud. My mouth tastes like metal. Several times a day, I think I'm about to pass out. On my way from my car to this doctor's office, I have to sit on the curb and rest briefly. Whenever I walk these days, it feels as if my legs belong to someone else, someone who has just run twelve marathons.

Again, the tests say I'm fine. Again, the doctor agrees with the tests. I'm too tired to put up a fight. On my way back to the car, I slump beside a manicured bush and cry.

~

I repeat this process six more times, with six more doctors. I get recommendations from anyone I know who has ever been sick. When the doctors all say the same thing, it feels as if my life is being written by Kafka in a super bad mood. My axis of understanding starts to shift. I've spent my entire life thinking that doctors are here to diagnose and treat, or at least diagnose, but no one has a term for my symptoms. The tests don't show anything, so I must be fine. Without a good alternative, I research my symptoms online.

I do not want to get medical advice from the World Wide Web; I am acutely aware of the perils of such a path. But what choice do I have, when all the professionals insist I'm tip-top? In addition to the fatigue and the sweating, I now have heart palpitations and painful pins and needles in the soles of my feet.

At night, while my boyfriend snores quietly, I scroll through pages in the half-light until four, five, six in the morning. I type as softly as I can, my pulse quickening as I connect dots from one medical article to the next and the next. I regret not having studied biochemistry in college. What good is *Madame Bovary* to me now? When my boyfriend stirs, I close the laptop and pretend to be asleep. My boyfriend, whose intelligence I respect deeply, thinks becoming your own doctor is a very, very bad idea. "I used to think the same thing," I tell him. "That's what everyone thinks, until this happens to them."

My friends in their smart-looking spectacles all side with my boyfriend. They are healthy. They do not understand. I'm already weary of not having a precise answer when people ask me what's wrong. I see it when their eyes say, *Well, you're standing up and talking; you must not be that sick.*

I am totally alone—*what's more isolating than illness?*—until I discover an entire subcontinent of the chronically ill within my computer. There are discussion boards, home remedies, support groups, YouTube videos. There are protocols to follow, links to online pharmacies where I can buy prescription drugs without a prescription.

I'm intrigued, repulsed, attracted, overwhelmed. I try to keep my wits as information flies at me from all directions. It's unfortunate that some of the articles employ bad grammar, cutesy fonts, squirrelly logic. The man in the YouTube videos appears to be missing some teeth. I try to overlook these things. Instead, I focus on the many aspects that ring true. *Finally*, I'm recognizing symptoms, identifying causes, reading about cures. My pulse throbs with new purpose. Maybe I'll be able to solve this thing on my own.

I buy a lot of supplements. I'm surprised by how many things will cure everything. Vitamin C cures everything. Iodine cures everything. Ozonated oil cures everything. I put everything that will cure everything in a blender, hit "Puree," and drink. I dub it a panacea smoothie and, laughing, ask my boyfriend, "Would you like some?" He would not.

I love my boyfriend; I think he is perhaps the Last of the Last Great Men. But his lack of enthusiasm for the world of amateur medicine is becoming a wedge. Whenever I share my discoveries, my theories, the fruits of my research, I can feel him doubting. He supports me in so many ways—cooking bone broth, juicing carrots, picking things up at the pharmacy—but inside, I know he doubts. "I want an official diagnosis as much as you do," I tell him. "But no one will give me one. What am I supposed to do, just crawl in a hole and keep praying?" My standard prayer has always been "May thy will be done," because I know my vision is partial, so I don't like to pray for specific outcomes. But this illness has tempted me to get a little more specific.

Before long, the kitchen cabinet is so full of supplements that it overflows. Rows of bottles cascade across the counter, creep up to the toaster oven. I have acquired so many supplements that I can no longer connect them all with their original purpose. I pick up a bottle of molybdenum, unscrew the cap, and sniff. I know molybdenum is good for something. *Sniff.* I just can't remember what. I put it back, concluding that molybdenum was never a great name for a supplement, anyway—it'd be much better for a body part. *What's wrong with me?* My molybdenum is broken.

I realize the psyche can influence the body, so I force myself to remain positive, keep an open mind. But one morning, I find myself peering through my new reading glasses at a supplement that claims to provide multidimensional immune system support. If it hadn't used the word *multidimensional,* I might have believed it had the power to support my immune system. But *multidimensional* is troubling. This supplement is likely bunk, yet I bought it, I'm holding it, I've been taking it for weeks.

In spite of my positive attitude, about a month later, my digestive system stops working. My intestines groan with absurdly audible explosions, gurgling and sloshing as if space aliens were building amusement parks, aqueducts, entire civilizations within my walls. All day and all night, they blast tunnels and run their water hoses. I want to press my boyfriend's ear to my belly, the way I might if I were pregnant. *Do you hear that? Can you even believe that?* I would ask. But I don't.

One clear, sunlit autumn morning, I wake up with excruciating abdominal pain, followed by a warm, flowing sensation. I wonder if there's a way to tell if I'm bleeding to death. I consider googling "symptoms of internal bleeding" but do not, because my hairdresser, while she was cutting what's left of my hair, told me the story of her cousin, who was found slumped over his keyboard, dead of a heart attack. The terms of his final Internet search still glowed on the screen. *Heart attack symptoms.* Now, I have an irrational fear that googling "symptoms of internal bleeding" will somehow precipitate a dire effect.

Besides, while the stabbing pain was unpleasant, the warm, flowing sensation is actually quite enjoyable. If there were a cure that enabled me to keep the warm, flowing feeling, but eliminate the stabbing, I would take it. But there is never such a cure in life. You buy both sides of the coin.

I try, absurdly, to talk myself out of being sick. *It's just anxiety,* I say. *It's psychosomatic. Try to focus on other things.* In front of my boyfriend, I pretend I'm doing a little better, and hope the pretense will slide into reality. But every day, I feel worse. It's as if my symptoms are accelerating.

My boyfriend comes home from writing at the library one afternoon to find me lying on the kitchen floor in the fetal position.

"What's wrong?" he asks.

"It feels like my organs are shutting down."

"Should I call the doctor?"

Instead of answering, I start to cry. I've already been to the doctors. They all say I'm fine.

My boyfriend squats beside me and takes my hand. To him this is a problem to be solved, plain and simple. He is a man of logic, of reason. I like this about him—it reminds me of my father.

"How can I help you?" he says, searching my face for clues. But I don't know the answer. I don't know what he can do. Eventually, the pain recedes, and he carries me to bed.

THE SLIDE

In the days and weeks that follow, things go sharply downhill. There are flashes of white light in my peripheral vision. I can't concentrate. My ears ring. I've always taken pride in my command of language, but I'm no longer in command. First I can't think of the word for *wall*. Then I call a toaster oven an oven toaster. I know what I mean, but my mouth says the other thing. I don't even realize my mistake until my boyfriend gives me a look.

Also, my emotions are beyond my control. When the dog barks, I react as if someone's stabbing me to death. One afternoon, when she barks for an hour straight, I tell her to please stop, that her barking is hurting my ears, but she only barks louder, so I yell at her to STOP, to STOP BARKING NOW, but she barks even more crazily, more constantly, until I finally grab her and squeeze her little body while I scream with the full force of my being, "Stop barking! Stop fucking barking! If you don't stop barking right now, I'm going to stop barking for you!" Afterward she cowers in the corner, afraid of me.

In the sickening silence that follows, I feel stunned. I feel poisoned. I am losing my very self. When I weep in the shower, lying helpless beneath the sharp needles of water, it is half pain and half fear.

I go to a garden and sit in the sun to try to get my head right. I attempt to meditate, even though I don't really know how it's done. I attempt to be still. I lack the will to pray. I don't know when I lost the feeling that someone was listening—that an omnipotent, loving presence attended to my every word. This could have been my faith's finest hour. Instead, in my center, in the warm nest where my faith used to sit, there's only a dull, throbbing fear.

While I wait in stillness, a plane passes overhead, riding the lavender clouds. I imagine it blowing up, chunks of flames and debris tumbling through the sky. I have these sorts of thoughts all the time now, out of nowhere. From my sunny garden bench, as I envision ash and scalding metal hurtling toward me, I wonder if I'd even bother to move out of the way.

On my walk home, the normal citizens of the world pass by, oblivious. The unsick wear their good health so cavalierly. They possess the most exquisite gift—an ermine cloak studded with magic gems—and they just drag it about, wiping their sweat with it. I used to do the same thing.

When my boyfriend asks how I'm doing, I hesitate to tell him the truth. I cry several times a day now—hot, helpless tears, like a child's. I do my best to act chipper when he's around, asking questions about his friends, his work. I don't want him to think I'm seeking attention; I don't want him to wonder if, on some unconscious level, I'm choosing this. But behind my smile, the ringing in my ears has grown constant now. Inside my head, there's malicious chatter, static, a live wire flailing about.

There's a crawling feeling beneath my skin. That part, I tell him. One night, after he showers and climbs into bed with a book, I whisper, "It's like having bedbugs, *on the inside*." There was a time when the things I whispered in my boyfriend's ear at this hour of night were of a decidedly different nature. As he turns the pages of his book, I can't tell if he's imperceptibly inching his body away.

After he clicks off the light, I lie in the fresh dark and ponder if I might have done something to bring about this suffering. My record is not without blemish. There was the time I stuffed a used maxi pad in the pocket of my little sister's parka. The time I was supposed to be driving home for Thanksgiving but I went to the movies with my boyfriend instead. There was the Hostess muffin incident. The cigarette fire in the woods. All the times I knew what was right, but followed my whims. Perhaps my lymph is clogged with the detritus of my mistakes. Maybe my own blood cries out against me.

CHIMERA

It turns out the culprit is not my blood; it's much more sinister. I find mold in my attic, mold in my basement, mold behind my walls. I've always thought that people who suffered from environmental illness were quacks, so this is karmic payback: now I'm one of them. My beloved house, with its wood-burning stove and wraparound deck and panoramic views of the lake—my house is as sick as I am. This house was my first major purchase in life, and when I bought it in February 1999, I felt so safe, so free, so much like an adult that after the moving truck drove away, I lay on the floor amid the stacks of boxes and cried.

Now the inspectors come in their protective clothing and show me all the types of mold I have, all the colors, where it hides. They do not use the phrase "toxic black mold," because all the colors of mold are toxic, they explain, and while I do not harbor every color of mold in my house, I have a wide variety, with especially high numbers for aspergillus.

I read everything that has ever been written about mold sickness. I study the inspectors' report. I talk to other people who've gone through the same thing—not Suzanne Somers, but the less famous people. There's a creeping conclusion I don't want to face, but ultimately, I do: I have to sell my house. Remediation often doesn't do the trick, once you've become sensitized to mold. Spores are microscopic—they reproduce, they hide. Like demons.

My friends in their smart-looking spectacles suggest, in a sideways sort of way, that I not disclose that my house has a hidden mold problem. But I disclose. I don't get a huge amount of money for the house, especially with the home-equity loan I have to pay off, but I get a small sum to tide us over. My boyfriend, my dog, and I move into a hotel—one of those hotels designed for extended residential stays. Our unit has a small living room and a kitchen.

In addition to losing my home, I must also lose all my possessions. Yes. Because if I bring my possessions with me, I'll contaminate the new environment. My possessions carry mycotoxins, which are the poisons mold uses to kill you, and they can't be washed out. I know all about mycotoxins now; I've become fluent in the horrors of mold sickness. I have a theory, actually, that mycotoxicosis is what killed Beethoven, and when I share it with the mold inspectors, they nod beneath their face masks, giving me the thumbs-up.

My boyfriend doesn't want to give away all his stuff. Naturally. But even he can see the mold, and he understands the concept of contagion. So his bed, his desk, his sleep sofa, his books, his clothes—he gives them all away.

This is love. Moved by his sacrifice, I take my boyfriend's hand. I tell him that being homeless, possessionless nomads will be an adventure. A chance for spiritual rebirth.

While my boyfriend supports the idea of spiritual rebirth on principle, he also points out that the two of us will be asked to leave the hotel as soon as our money runs out. I haven't been doing much freelance copyediting; he hasn't been doing much freelance web design.

I tell him there are options. I've read about moldies who camp in their backyards, squat in trailer parks, live in their cars. So many live in their cars, in fact, that I wonder why some savvy company hasn't designed a sedan fully equipped with blackout curtains, seats that recline to a bed, and a refrigerated glove box. What a hit that'd be!

My boyfriend isn't so sure that'd be a hit. He isn't so sure about any of this. I look into his eyes and tell him I'm ready for whatever the crazy adventure brings. I'll live in a tepee; I'll eat cold beans from a can. I just want to feel normal again.

There's a doctor in a nearby town who specializes in mold sickness. She's very expensive, and insurance doesn't cover it, but what price health? I expect to feel elated—after so many months, to finally know what's wrong, to be under a professional's care—but a disturbing uncertainty threads through me while she speaks. I do not like that her bra strap is showing. I do not like that she spends half the appointment trying to get her air conditioner to work. I do not like that her hair flies in all directions and there's nary a white coat in sight.

From my chair, I upbraid myself. I know better than to judge things superficially—has this illness taught me nothing if not that? Or have I forgotten all those white coats who insisted I was 100 percent? I shift my focus from the bra strap and, instead, remind myself that throughout the ages, there has never been any indication that wisdom favors the well groomed. On the contrary, wasn't it the wild-haired locust eaters who spoke truth?

When she finally gets her A/C to work, the mold doctor has me fill out one of those forms with little boxes to check for my symptoms. I begin ticking off boxes furiously, but there are so many symptoms for which there is no box.

Utterly famished but no appetite.
Utterly fatigued but can't sleep.
Fear and trepidation where soul should be.
Celestial loneliness.

The mold doctor takes my list and settles in behind her desk. She tells me stories about herself as much as she asks questions about my health. She started out in Infectious Disease, she was a superstar at Johns Hopkins, AIDS is not what we all think it is. She seems wacky. My new friend from the Internet has told me that mold doctors are sometimes a little wacky because they often start out as moldies themselves.

When she launches into another anecdote about her days at Johns Hopkins, I interrupt. "It feels as if I'm dying, as if my organs are melting, as if I'm slipping away in plain sight, and no one believes me."

The mold doctor believes me. She promises to help me rid myself of mold. She's going to prescribe two powerful antifungal drugs, and for the next six months, I'm to spend three hours every day on my back, dripping them up my nostrils. But first, I must stop eating carbohydrates.

In my mind, even as she speaks, I sever all carbohydrates from my life. I will never touch a noodle again. She seems to expect resistance, but there's none. "That's fine," I tell her, leaning forward. "I've been ill and in pain for over a year. I'm at the end of my rope. I'll do anything." The mold doctor nods, understanding. Then, in a musty exam room, without having me change into a gown, she touches a few pressure points, probes my liver, and orders some tests. I leave her office and go home to my hotel room, feeling more optimistic than I have in months.

With my newfound hope, I become intimately acquainted with fungicidal drugs such as Sporanox and amphotericin B, fungicidal substances such as artemisinin and oregano and GSE, toxin binders such as modified citrus pectin and cholestyramine. Boxes of medication arrive weekly, packed on dry ice. My refrigerator is full of syringes.

As promised, I eschew all carbohydrates. But I can't help it if I dream of them. At night, the scrim of my unconscious dances with chocolate cake and cherries, whipped cream and wine. Buttered French toast with warm maple syrup. Is there anything better? Now that I've been officially prohibited from interacting with carbohydrates,

carbohydrates are all I see. I notice that people eat them right out in the open, walking down the street. *Is this legal? Has this always happened?* Overnight, I've developed a superhuman ability to spot a muffin at a thousand yards. Men, women, and babies consume carbohydrates carelessly, mindlessly, while driving cars, while bobbing in their buggies. Life is a carbohydrate orgy.

Meanwhile, I spend much of that spring on my back, with an absurdly large syringe positioned at my upturned nostril.

One day, my college roommate calls to say she's coming through town and would like to stay with us. She wants to meet the fabulous, fabled boyfriend. If we have a residential hotel suite, she says, why not share? When she gets here, she seems angry that I'm not eating carbohydrates. "You're already so thin!"

I tell her this isn't a diet, I'm doing it on doctor's orders. I look into her face as I explain that, for the past eighteen months, I've been desperately, mysteriously ill. I point to the dark circles under my eyes, my thinning hair.

My college roommate is a lifelong dieter; she's very competitive; she doesn't understand. The fact that I'm thin now is a threat to her. She begins to monitor what I eat, and comment on it. Then she starts monitoring what the dog eats. In her opinion, I am eating too little, and the dog is eating too much.

She's focusing on all the wrong things. But I can't think of a way to tell her this without hurting her feelings. When we go out to dinner at an Indian restaurant, I try to explain what it's like to feel judged at the exact moment I most need to feel supported.

Without asking, she slops a spoonful of *saag paneer* onto my plate. Staring at the soggy lumps of green cheese, I realize something. My college roommate is a bit of a bully. She has always bullied me, and I have always let myself be bullied. It's an interesting realization to have, even if I don't have the strength to do anything about it.

The next morning, on my way to the shower, I find my college room-mate unspooling her yoga mat in the hall. Before commencing she has fixed herself a Bellini with the leftover champagne—a ritual she refers to as a "pretox."

I like this side of my room-mate. From her yoga mat, she looks like a delicate, origami bird. With her mouth near her knees, she asks me, "What's it like to have lost everything you own, to be freed from the shackles of the material world?"

I tell her it feels liberating and exhilarating, the way I imagine skydiving must feel.

She sips her Bellini and strikes a new pose that looks storklike. "Illness," she says, "is a teacher." And I wonder, again, what my illness might be trying to teach.

From my spot in the hallway, I invite the answers to come. If I were on speaking terms with God, I might be tempted to say, *Look. I know I must've seemed a little distracted before, what with all that fun I used to have and all those carbs I used to eat. But whatever it is you want me to understand, I'm listening.*

I cock my head, my ear to the shell of the universe. But the universe doesn't answer.

That night, I wake from a dream that I'm back together with my college boyfriend. I haven't dreamed of him in a decade; it must be a free association with my roommate. Despite that, I send him a message on Facebook: "I dreamed we were shagging again. It was nice." *Shagging?* What am I doing? It doesn't even sound like something I'd say.

Instead of going back to sleep, I stare at the patches of skin on my calves where my muscles twitch and pulse, unprompted. I know that these twitches are called fasciculations, that they're linked with Lou Gehrig's disease. I think of my father, whose shirt-collar size kept increasing for a full year before he even knew he was sick. When I hear my roommate shuffling toward the bathroom, I ask in a soft voice:

"Am I dying?"

"You're not dying."

"I know, but are my organs shutting down?"

"They're not shutting down."

"How do you know?"

"You're going to get better. Trust me."

But I don't get better.

For six months, I religiously follow everything the mold doctor tells me to do. But nothing changes. I don't improve from being out of the moldy house; I don't respond to the cholestyramine or Sporanox or amphotericin B. I still feel exhausted, in pain, and incapable of thinking clearly. When I request genetic testing, it turns out I don't have any of the "mold genes" that make some people especially vulnerable to mycotoxins. Beethoven likely died of mold sickness, but it's not what's killing me. I'm back at square one—an illness without a diagnosis, an executioner without a face.

WAGING A WAR

The Internet thinks I have parasites. My swollen belly, my bulging eyes, my dramatic twenty-five-pound weight loss—they all point to the presence of worms or amoebas in my gut. These crafty critters are eating my food, they're crapping in my bloodstream, they are what's destroying me.

Ha! I think. My original instincts about space aliens were not that far off. We all have parasites, the Internet says, trying to make me feel better. But in some people, they overgrow. *Some people,* I think, *are too nice.*

I sit in my hotel bed in a worklike pose, but I do not do any actual work. As a freelancer, if I do not do any actual work, I do not get any actual pay. But I have lost all interest in punctuation. Instead, I study parasites day and night, their hoary photographs and slimy habits. I try to determine which one I have. It's not unlike choosing a pet. I read about their origins, their tendencies; I try to envision this foreign creature in relationship to myself.

I bring my face right up to the screen so I can stare into a nematode's vacant eyes.

Could you be living inside me?

When my boyfriend walks in, I slam the laptop shut.

"What are you doing?"

"Nothing."

"Are you pretending to be a doctor?"

"No."

"Then why do you look all excited and sweaty, like you do when you read about medical stuff?"

I let that pass without comment.

"I'm making steak with organic vegetable stew for dinner," he says. Before he leaves, he stops. "For God's sake, would you go see a professional?"

Once he's gone, I realize he's right. How can I treat a parasitic infection when I don't know which parasite I have? They all respond to different drugs. I don't own a lab; I don't know CPT codes. I need the professionals.

On my way to yet another doctor's office, I tell myself this is optimism; it's the sensible thing to do. But in the pit of my stomach, I feel as I did when I sped over the Tobin Bridge at three in the morning to temporarily reconcile with a doomed boyfriend. Mainstream medicine is like a bad lover I keep running back to, even though I know he can't give me what I need.

At the Infectious Disease specialist, the team of doctors refuses to test me for parasites. They will not test me unless I have recently traveled to Africa or have lived in Asia for ten years or more. "Please," I beg. "I'll do anything—I'll be part of an experimental trial. I'll pay for the tests myself."

"No," they say. They will not test me; I will not pay. I've read that nearly all American doctors are in inexplicable, collective denial on the subject of parasites, but until this moment, I hadn't believed it.

I keep my lower lip from quivering. Crying will only make things worse. "But what about my dog?" I ask. "My dog, who likes to nap with her butt against my pillow? My dog, who had two different types of parasites when she arrived, one helminthic and one protozoan—tapeworms and giardia? How'd she get them? Has my dog been traveling to Africa without me?"

They do not answer. They do not care about my dog. "You may leave now," they say, and show me the door.

When I get home, my boyfriend hands me a glass of fresh-pressed carrot juice with a sprig of mint. He squeezes my shoulders and informs me that my favorite musician is playing a free outdoor concert two blocks away from our hotel.

I long to go, but, instead, I crawl into bed. I try to explain that, unfortunately, I spent what little energy I had chasing after doctors who refuse to help me.

After he cooks me a free-range grass-fed steak that I don't have the stomach to eat, my boyfriend goes to hear my favorite musician without me. I'm glad. I feel bad for all the ways my illness has hemmed him in.

As soon as he closes the door, I open my computer.

The Internet offers omnibus solutions for parasites. There is diatomaceous earth, there is horse dewormer, there is turpentine. I try all of them. That's right. I, who all my life have been loath to take baby aspirin—I eat horse dewormer with a spoon; I drink turpentine from a plastic cup. In the course of two years, I've become not only someone I no longer recognize, but someone I previously wouldn't have trusted to vacuum my car. At the outset, I was desperate. Now, I don't know what to call it.

In addition to the horse dewormer and the turpentine, the Internet offers other remedies, ones that sound less life-threatening. Jumping on a miniature trampoline will get my lymph flowing again, so I buy a rebounder. Swishing coconut oil in my mouth for twenty minutes a day will pull toxins from my body, so I order a jar. Coffee enemas will cleanse my liver, so I purchase bucket, bag, and hose. Soon there are so many treatments in the queue, I wonder how I'll even have time to employ them all.

The concept of the coffee enema at first mystifies me. I'm all for drinking coffee out of a cup, but it never would have occurred to me to stick it anywhere else.

The dog, too, does not comprehend the coffee enema. She sees me with nose to the floor, down on all fours—naturally, she thinks it's party time. When I explain, in a pinched voice, "No party. Party later," her tilted head makes me laugh. Then, as my intestines seize, I stop laughing. The dog jams her nose into my cheekbone and rolls onto her back, inviting me to rub her belly.

One ingenious afternoon, I decide to bounce on the rebounder while retaining a coffee enema and simultaneously oil swishing. I do this while my boyfriend is not around. I think of it not as the final peg in my mental collapse, but as clever time management. When the coffee enema proves capable of eliciting ever more sudden urges, I slide the rebounder into the bathroom. This way, I'll be closer to the commode. Also, it might help if I were naked. When my boyfriend gets home, I'll have to explain why there's now a trampoline in the bathroom and I'm down on all fours, scrubbing the toilet, naked. But maybe he won't notice. Lately, when I look at him, he seems only halfway there. When I talk, he seems to only halfway listen.

When he finds the turpentine, and I admit I'm drinking it, my boyfriend is appalled. Somehow, explaining that "other people are doing it, on the Internet," does not help my case. Part of the argument that follows centers on a fact I've recently learned: if one person in a household has parasites, all the people in the household have parasites, and if one person's being treated, all the people have to be treated. Otherwise, the sick person will never get well. Parasites are catchy. People pass them back and forth.

My boyfriend doesn't want to hear this. He will not be drinking any turpentine. He doesn't want to hear any of it, he tells me.

"Well, I don't want to hear it, either. Only, guess what? I have to hear it—I'm *living* it—I'm trapped inside this nightmare while you're off listening to music and eating carbohydrates!

"You eat a lot of sushi," I tell him, knowingly. Maybe he's the one with parasites. Maybe he gave them to me.

There's a word for the look on my boyfriend's face, but I'm not sure if it's *contempt* or *disgust*.

Before he climbs into bed that night, my boyfriend pauses beside a photograph of the two of us kayaking on the lake by our old house. The sun sparkles on the water, my hair, my eyes. My arms are not emaciated; my smile brims. "Things were so . . . different then," he says, and I try, and mostly succeed, not to hear this as *I liked you better before you got sick*. I try not to think, *So this is what it feels like to lose everything.*

FLATLINING

I call my college roommate and explain that I've become even more desperate, more of whatever the nameless thing is that comes after desperation. I tell her that lately, for no reason, I sometimes imagine plucking my own eyes out. Just fitting a letter opener at the lower rim and wielding it like a lever. This is especially bizarre because I've always liked my eyes; my eyes may be my best feature. I push the thoughts away, into the bin with the exploding planes and all of the other disturbing thoughts that plague me. But they push back. One minute, I'll be ordering a magnetic clay detox bath off the Internet, the next minute—BAM!—letter opener in my eye. It's distracting. I'm worried I might be possessed.

I hear little grunts and groans on the other end of the line, and I imagine my roommate on her yoga mat, cradling the cell phone between her ankles. "I can't really talk now," she says, but she will bestow a helpful nugget. "Sometimes it's hard to know the difference between a religious experience and bad potato salad." Also, she knows someone who was helped by a Russian guy, a hypnotist or something. He lives in Brookline.

I find and go to the Russian healer, the one who has cured famous people of their phobias and addictions. The little girl in me still trusts the ancient stories where people were healed by a laying of hands or the strategic placement of mud and spittle, so I arrive with an open heart, genuinely ready for my miracle. There are twenty of us in the room, seated in a semicircle. The air-conditioning is on so high that it's difficult to concentrate. On top of that, I'm having a hard time understanding the Russian through his accent. He has something to say about Rembrandt, which I gather because he's holding Rembrandt's bust, but I don't catch what it is. Is he saying that he healed Rembrandt? Has he had several lives?

My openheartedness is wavering. If the space felt less like an arctic prison, I might feel more cellularly inclined to be healed.

The Russian explains that we need not believe in his technique in order for it to work. This seems handy, under the circumstances. I'm seated at the front, near his desk. He walks over and asks me to feel the strength of his calf muscle. I'm not sure if this is part of the healing process. *Do I have to?* Also I don't know if it'd be rude to ask him to turn up the heat. Usually I don't go anywhere without the throw I bought at Crate & Barrel that I pretend is a shawl, but of course today I left my blankie in the car, and I've intuitively sensed, as on the first day of kindergarten, that trips to the outside world are now forbidden.

The Russian is waiting. After I squeeze his calf and pretend to be impressed, I scan the room for unemployed sweatshirts, shawls, or blankets. If I spot one, when the Russian isn't looking, I plan to use a makeshift stranger-to-stranger sign language to ask its owner if I may borrow it.

But there are no unemployed sweatshirts—these people don't want to die of hypothermia any more than I do—and there is no healing miracle. At the end of his presentation, the Russian presses his thumb into the center of each of our foreheads, presumably to impart some sort of psychic strength, but I receive nothing.

When I call her to report on the lackluster, frigid experience, my roommate has more ideas. Yes, I've been living in a hotel and not working. Yes, bankruptcy looms. But I should check out that new spa over on Newbury Street. They have an amazing acupuncturist.

I've never had acupuncture before, and I'm a bit wary, but it doesn't hurt. The Chinese woman also practices something called Reiki, and asks if I'd like to try it. Reiki is not what I came here for, but sure, if she wants to Reiki me, have at it.

The Reiki doesn't hurt, either. But my massage requires some preparatory instructions that the acu-massa-Reikist doesn't understand at first.

"What most people like when they get a massage," I say, "hurts. I need it to be very soft. Light. Gentle. Yes?"

I repeat this a few times, but it's only when I demonstrate on her arm that she gets it.

"Ahhhh," she says. "Like baby!"

"Yes. Like baby."

As she works her hands over me, she tells me my chi is very weak.

"I know," I say. My chi is having a little nap. My chi is on vacation.

In addition to my chi deficiency, she says there's not a lot going on with my spleen.

I wonder if my spleen could be pouting. I talk to my spleen. I apologize. I explain that whatever I did, I certainly didn't mean it, and the same goes for the rest of my organs in there. I know they work very hard for me, day in and day out, and have for a long time, and I've never even thanked them. And, well . . . I'm thanking them now. I'm aware that there's exquisite machinery inside me, performing all kinds of essential tasks, and it obviously needs something; I just don't know what.

Although I make every kind of effort imaginable, my attempts at alternative therapies fail. The Reiki and the acupuncture, the oil swishing and the enemas, the diet and meditation and massage—they all do nothing. I am as sick as ever. I wake up every day in a fog of confusion and pain, drenched in sweat with zero energy. I've lost everything I

HYSTERIA

Since all hope has been crossed off, I opt not to go on the trip to Europe that my boyfriend and I had planned together, the nonrefundable trip we paid for a year ago, before we both went broke. Instead, while he's in Paris, I go to the emergency room of one of the finest hospitals in the country. I bring with me, in a sealed Ziploc inside another sealed Ziploc inside a paper bag, the worm I just scooped from the toilet with a disposable fork. In spite of myself, in spite of the unpleasantness of it, I feel proud of this worm. This worm is going to be my redemption.

At the ER, I wait for hours, with every breath inhaling the tubercular coughs of my fellow infirm. Eventually, the white coats emerge to inform me that my worm has tested negative for parasites. I stare, uncomprehending; they have to repeat themselves. When I finally understand, it's hilarious. It's better than the comedy of Steven Wright. Glancing around, I wonder about hidden cameras. Could *Steven Wright* be behind this?

When my boyfriend gets back from Europe, he looks at me differently—a look that suggests he's been in the presence of other women, Parisian women in long black dresses who smell like roses and do not talk about parasites. My boyfriend has been doing some thinking while he was away. He insists I see a psychiatrist.

I have no time for his condescending ultimatums. Seeing a psychiatrist is not what I need to do. I know what I need to do. I have a plan; I was just waiting for him to come back from Europe to implement it.

While I speak, I begin to get dressed. Although it's the middle of the afternoon, I'm still in my nightgown. I yank on jeans and a jacket without taking the nightgown off. When I'm finished, the pink and brown flannel flowers hang down to my knees.

"I'm going back to the Infectious Disease specialist. When I get there, I'm going to insist that they test me for parasites. I won't leave until they do. If I have to, I'll handcuff myself to a chair, or a table, or whatever there is that might recommend itself for handcuffing."

As I approach him, my boyfriend instinctively backs away. I hold out my phone.

"I need you to film it."

"No," he says, shaking his head. "No." He wants no part of this.

"Yes," I say. "I need your help. I was just waiting for you to come back. They'll be less likely to dismiss me if they know they're being filmed, and I can't film it myself. We need to go. Now."

I yank on a pom-pom wool hat, even though it's not wool-hat weather. By now, I've learned that they keep hospitals as cold as the Russian's living room.

When I reach the door, I turn around. My boyfriend is staring at me in my wool hat and my nightgown. There are no words for his expression. Or there may be a word, but I don't know it anymore.

"Come on," I say. "We need to do this now."

"Do you even see yourself? Do you even know what you're doing?"

"I know what I'm doing. I'm going to the Infectious Disease specialist. I need them to test me for parasites."

"You need help."

"You're right. I need help! And I'm asking you to help me. Will you help me in my hour of need or not?" I look him in the eye. I maintain a level gaze.

"This is insane," my boyfriend says, little bulbs of muscle rising at his jawline. "You aren't going about this the right way."

"Oh, the *right* way? The *right* way? And what exactly is *the right way*? Tell me one fucking way I haven't tried!"

Hot tears lace my cheeks. I cover my face. "I'm sick," I say, "and no one will help me. I'm begging you—I've never asked you for anything—I'm only asking you for this one small thing. If you've ever cared about me at all. Please."

My boyfriend walks over and squares my shoulders. He holds me at arm's length, his pupils wide. His gaze strains to transmit some message, but I don't grasp what it is.

"I'm so sorry this has happened to you," he says, and his voice catches. "I really am. But I can't be part of it anymore. Do you understand?"

"I know you're leaving," I say, suddenly calm. "I've known it for weeks. Please. Just help me do this one thing before you walk away."

He lets go of my shoulders. "I'm not walking away. You're pushing me."

"You're a coward!" I say, spittle escaping my lips. "You care so much what other people think! That's why you won't help me with this!"

"You're out of your mind," he says. "You don't even know what you're saying."

"I'm not crazy!" I scream. "You keep trying to tell me I'm crazy, but I'm not! You're not even on my side—you're against me! You've been against me this whole time! Why would I even want to stay with someone who's against me? The only crazy thing about me is that I'm still with you!"

"This is what you should be filming," my boyfriend says. "*This.*"

Something snaps then, some battered thing inside me finally shatters, breaks into a thousand glimmering shards, and I cry, screaming, wild-eyed, at the Last of the Last Great Men. The bile at the back of my throat, the chatter in my head, the desperate drive in the pit of my gut—I employ them all in his direction. I am consumed.

When I run out of breath, I grab my purse, slam the door, and race for the hospital.

On my way, I try to compose myself. If I arrive sobbing and hysterical, they'll focus solely on the crazy, instead of on the parasites that are causing it. I cannot be that woman.

At the hospital, things go much as they did with my boyfriend. They believe I'm going about this the wrong way; they would like me to put away my camera. Because the words are fresh on my tongue, and because it's true, I tell them I have never asked them for anything, I'm only asking for this one small thing. I do not actually own handcuffs, but, nonetheless, I refuse to leave. "I'm sick," I tell them. "Can't you see that I'm sick and desperate and afraid? I just need someone to listen. To help me. Please." And of all the things I've said today, this is the most true.

They call the security guards. I'm surprised they think they need five. The security guards are not thugs; they let me talk, but, eventually, they insist I leave. "I'm not leaving," I say. In spite of myself, I start to cry. I cycle through three phrases as they each take their turn trying to convince me: "I'm sick. I won't go. You can't make me." These three phrases are what I'm still mumbling, hours later, when I stand and shuffle for the exit. "I'm sick. I won't go. You can't make me," I whisper. Stumbling, crying, half blind.

On my way home, my thoughts turn inward. We all bear our share of suffering; this portion must be my share. Somehow, in the course of my life, I must have used up all my luck and cosmic goodwill. There was the time I called my mother a bitch on Christmas Day. The time in high school—several times—when I stole a hundred-dollar bill from her purse. There was the painting my little sister made of a dove—perfect, wings outstretched beneath a violet moon—that I snatched and ripped to shreds. There was the summer I loved a married man. The semester I copied my friend's answers to the math problem sets. The baby I could have had, but didn't.

~

When I get home, my boyfriend has a duffel bag on the bed and is packing it. While he speaks, my mind travels back to a day by the lake when we kayaked and drank wine and read poetry together. The smooth glassy surface of the lake, the tart lime shrimp, the sight of him in his flip-flops. I don't blame him for leaving. If roles had been reversed, I don't know if I'd have stuck around this long.

The next morning, while the sun brightly shines, I watch him walk out of my life. Before he leaves, we hug each other and whisper "I love you" and cry. Just before he exits, as he reaches the door, he stops, turns around, and smiles. With his eyes flooded with tears, he presses his fingers to his lips and raises his hand high, his face shining.

I have kept my life small. I had the Last of the Last Great Men. I have my dog. I have kept my life small to protect myself. But, still, pain has found me.

SURRENDER

A week after the breakup, I find myself driving through the town where I went to college. It's a place designed more for walking, a convoluted grid of one-way streets, and driving it can be disorienting. I go around and around, in figure-eights, circling infinity. Being back in my college town after so many years away feels familiar yet foreign, which is exactly the way I feel to myself. Charlie's Kitchen is still there, but the Wursthaus is now a bank. There seem to be a lot of banks.

I've always liked how it feels to be in a car, to be in motion with a view, so I keep going. I want my body to remember what it was like before it got sick. I wend my way through Massachusetts, taking a driving tour of my youth, and end up near my childhood home.

At an intersection, I look up and see the supermarket where my family used to shop. I park and go inside. It's a Whole Foods now, but the music's the same. All the speakers are tuned to a ballad by Journey— "Faithfully." Hearing it's like being spritzed with a perfume called High School. I used to love this song, and I wish I could remember what it felt like to hear it back then. There was a boy; I remember that. There was a boy named John, who played lacrosse, and I used to listen to this song on my Walkman on the way to his games. Or maybe I listened to it on the way to a school ski trip? Some of the details are gauzy, but that boy loved me; that much I'm sure of. John's love was a globe of light, keeping me safe. I would've gone anywhere with him, done anything. I was so carefree then, so innocent. Things were so . . . different.

The song ends.

The overhead lights are blinding. The other carts make a murderous squall. I'm lost. It's obscenely cold. My blood contracts, my vision a swarm of bleached spots.

Staggering, I realize I'm about to pass out. I grasp the handle of a nearby cart as shoppers continue to push past me, ferrying their frozen peas. Other people stride so forcefully. They exist with such conviction.

When I was little, they used to sell stuffed animals at this supermarket, but they don't have them here anymore. One morning, I stood ogling the pile, my fingers hooked over the metal bin, my father by my side. He said I could choose whichever one I wanted, and I plucked a striped tiger from the lot, cradling her throughout the store, and named her Tiger Lily. Later, when she developed a tear along one of her seams, I tried to fix her up with Popsicle sticks and dental floss, but my attempts to heal her ruined her instead.

I do not stand in the frozen-foods aisle and cry. The whole supermarket is preposterously cold; the last thing I want to do is spend extra time in frozen foods. Instead, I look for something to buy, something I would've liked as a child—a packaged cherry pie, perhaps. I won't be able to eat it, but I can look at it; I can recall its satisfying heft. I steer my cart away from the section where they sell supplements. Maybe I'll get a bottle of water—water's safe. Except for the fact that it comes in plastic. But I try not to think about that.

In the checkout line, when it's my turn, I feel weirdly overwhelmed by the speed of the conveyor belt. I find myself saying to the gum-chewing teenager: "Slow the belt down! Shut the belt off!" Then I add, "Why is it so fucking cold in here?"

Exiting the parking lot, I try to ignore the Miata behind me that's honking incessantly. The flow of traffic didn't used to be set up like this when I was a kid, and I can't figure out how to get back on the road. There's a sign saying it's a one-way street, but then there's an arrow pointing in the other direction. It's confusing. The Miata behind me honks again. My hands and feet are sweating. Suddenly it swerves around me, tires screeching, as the driver sticks out his fist and gives me the finger.

I have never been more alone.

Driving home from my childhood supermarket that's now a Whole Foods, I feel disoriented. The passage of time is baffling me. I remember so clearly the summer I watched a religious thriller at a multiplex in Queens and drank black coffee at Diamond Dave's in Iowa City and made love with my boyfriend in the tall grass beside the high school and sliced open my big toe on a broken shell at Cape Cod. How could each of those things possibly have been ten, twenty, thirty, forty years ago?

I go to the center of the city. I sit on the steps of the big church, across from the public library. It's a glorious autumn afternoon. The descending sun floods the buildings with a yellow light that's supersaturated, and the adjacent shadows are supersaturated, too. The whole world is chiaroscuro. There's a glass building across from me that doubles the beauty.

I used to love days like this. October in New England used to be my favorite time of year. I still love it, but I can't feel it anymore. That joy, those currents of affection that used to course through me—where'd they go? After losing every other thing, must I lose that, too?

I remain still. I stay calm. I do not contemplate the specter of a life without joy. I do not feel the full weight of my endless, numbered days. All those people on the Internet, pouring out their ailments and their sorrow. I understand now—understand a little—what they meant.

It's five o'clock, and the workaday world is heading home at full speed. It swirls past me, blind to me, but I don't feel alone. I feel deeply connected; it's just that the people I feel connected to are the dead and the dying, the ones who are already slipping away, joining the chiaroscuro light. The light is alive—I know. I sense its energy; it tugs at my womb like a tide.

If only I could disappear. If only I could let everything go. It's not exactly that I want to die. I just want the suffering to be over.

I need to be able to see the sky better. Seeing the sky better might make things right.

I descend the steps of the church, go to the middle of the sidewalk, and lie down. Passersby shoot me disapproving looks, but that's all right. What'd their approval ever do for me when I had it? I lost my health, my love, my home, my bank account, all while they blithely smiled.

Staring up at the sky, I close my eyes, touch my fingers to my lips, and raise my hand high. It feels as if I'm saying goodbye to something; I just don't know what.

There will come a day, a few months from now, when I will find out what's been making me ill. It will be a word I've never heard before, and when I hear this word, and learn what causes it and what can be done to cure it, everything will finally begin to make sense.

But here, on this glorious autumn afternoon, in the middle of the sidewalk, none of this has happened yet. I do not yet know the word for what's wrong; I have no idea that a diagnosis and successful treatment are winging toward me. All I know is the supersaturated light, the impassive pavement, the sooty boots of passersby.

And because I do not know what's coming, I am unable to realize that in this very moment, as I lie here hopeless and hollow in spite of good news just around the bend, I am experiencing the archetypal handicap of my species, its one true ailment: I am blind to the future—but I can see the past, and I see it with such fierce clarity that my eyes flick open.

All my life, I've been a pushover. From that very first slap, the world has bullied me, and I have let myself be bullied. But no more. I will not be too nice. I will not muzzle the truth. I will say: *You are mistaken.* I will tell them: *You are focusing on all the wrong things.* There is a voice that lives inside my head. I will give it breath.

My tears make the air sparkle. The static crackles; someone is listening; I sense a hidden joke.

Well, *yes*, I admit. People might be less inclined to walk all over me if I didn't lie down in footpaths. But, still. I will not be made to feel ashamed. I will not cower in silence. I will learn to stride forcefully like everybody else. And I will find my answers—they can't stop me; I won't let them. I will keep on searching, in spite of endless obstacles, a broken body, a ruined heart. I will search until I am blind and mute and paralyzed—and even then, I will search.

Because children see nothing wrong with lying in the middle of the sidewalk during rush hour, a little girl has approached. She stands over me, the back of her hand shielding her eyes.

"What are you doing?"

"Trying to feel better."

"Are you sick?"

"Yes."

"You don't look sick."

I laugh. It's preferable to hear it spoken aloud instead of feeling people think it. "I don't look sick. But I am."

"What's wrong with you?"

"Nobody knows."

The little girl sucks her lip, pondering this.

I can't help but notice her good health—her ruddy cheeks, her pudgy calves. *Please God,* I pray, as if she were my own. *Protect her, keep her safe.*

A cloud crosses the sun, and I can see her more clearly now—there's a jagged scar beneath her chin.

The wind picks up, and all at once every atom of the city is in motion—clouds shifting, leaves scattering, the river of people branching by. When she kneels beside me, the girl and I form a stationary island, a still point in the endless throng. The air feels weightless as she opens her mouth.

"I was sick once, too. But I'm better now."

PART IV

MIRACLE

In your twenties, you have a problem. You'd like to be a writer, but you don't know how to write. In fact, even though you've been alive for more than two decades, you don't know how to do a lot of things, including pay your bills, file your taxes, or feed yourself properly. But you know you have something to say, and you've heard about a prestigious writing competition through some college classmates, so you spend hours at your computer, punching keys. You want to make something full of heart, but not sentimental; smart, but not esoteric; suspenseful, but literary. It's a tall order, and you don't have a clue how to start. You carry a tape recorder with you everywhere so that, no matter where you go—to the airport or the doctor or your grandmother's house—you're always watching, learning, taking notes. Some part of you is always sculpting sentences in your head.

The deadline for the prestigious writing competition arrives, so you try to print out what you've made, this lopsided thing you've stitched together out of hope and pain and dental floss, but, of course, your printer doesn't work—nothing in the tech department ever worked for you in those days—so you have to put your thing on a thumb drive and rush to the Kinko's down the block and print it out there, with the help of the Kinko's guy, of course, because even at a place that's all about printing, that's *only* about printing, you still can't get the %#$&@ printer to work. Then, you frantically stick your printout in an envelope and race to the post office.

The contest deadline is midnight on December 31, so, of course, you show up at the all-night post office across from Madison Square Garden at 11:58 on New Year's Eve. You aren't expecting other people to actually have *postal needs* at that hour, but they do, so you miss the deadline by a few seconds. Thirty-two seconds, to be exact.

You try to get the nice lady behind the counter to maybe stamp your envelope with a time that's a minute earlier, but, no, the post office is a federal institution, the Feds don't do things like that, and *could you please move it along, miss*—these other people in line have cocktails to drink once they meet their postal needs.

After you leave the building, you stand alone on the stone steps under the enormous inscription,

Neither snow nor rain nor heat nor gloom of night stays these couriers from the swift completion of their appointed rounds, feeling disappointed in everything, especially yourself. And when it starts to snow, you start to cry.

A postman in his trim blue cap comes bounding up the steps—which you guess makes sense, 'cause that's where he works—and when he asks what's wrong, you tell him about the contest you aren't going to win, how you squandered your chance at even being considered, you've been a complete idiot, yet again, the recurring theme of your whole idiotic life. You look up at him with your tear-streaked face and say: "I only missed it by a few seconds. If only I'd gotten here one minute sooner."

The postman waits until you're finished before he speaks.

"Honey," he says, flashing his big postman grin, "when it *ain't* your time, you can't *make* it happen. And when it *is* your time, you can't *stop* it."

You—you like that. You like that so much it even becomes your mantra for a while. But before long, you find yourself wondering: *Well . . . when's it going to be my time?*

Because it seems as if everything around you in those years is designed to accentuate the sense of impatience and longing that's building up inside you.

You watch a baseball game and think: *When do I get to have an at bat?* Or you go to a Broadway show and wonder: *When do I get to sing my heart out?* Everything you want feels utterly palpable yet completely out of reach.

And it's difficult, because while this is happening, it seems that all manner of success is being visited upon every single one of your friends. It's as if you're all in a giant pile of fireworks, and your friends' lives are the *fabulous yellow roman candles exploding like spiders across the stars.* While your life is . . . a bag of cat litter.

Five years go by. Then ten. Then twenty. And then, something terrible happens. Your sister Melissa's husband gets sick, really sick, where on a Friday he feels like he's coming down with the flu, and by Monday a staph infection in his blood has made him septic and all his organs are shutting down. And the doctors have to try to explain to your sister that her husband of ten years and the father of their four small children is maybe going to die.

So you pray. You pray as hard as you can— harder than you ever have for anything else in your life—and you ask everyone you know to pray for a miracle. A *real* miracle.

But you don't get it. David dies, and you can't believe it. You still can't believe it. You don't think you will ever fully believe or understand how it is that one person is given ninety-six years, and another only thirty-seven years. Or ten years. Or one week. Or one day.

But after David dies, your perspective on so many things changes—including that girl crying on the steps of the all-night post office on New Year's Eve. You used to think she was an incompetent loser who needed an alarm clock, an MFA, and possibly a slap in the face. But now, you look back at her as if from very far away, a distance greater than years, and you think: *Look. You'd discovered the thing that makes you you. You had taken the truth of your heart and put it on a piece of paper and put a stamp on it. You had found your dream, and you were chasing after it with both hands. That was your time; you just didn't see it. It's always our time. That's the miracle.*

DIAGNOSES

After my boyfriend leaves, things rapidly unravel. Plants die, mail piles up, dishes go unwashed. Not since I had mono in my senior year of college have I been so conscious of the massive amount of energy it takes to do even minuscule tasks. Folding a pile of laundry feels like a herculean achievement. The central energy-producing engine of my body seems to have completely shut down; it's not uncommon for me to spend eighteen hours a day in bed.

One bright afternoon, awake but still motionless in my not entirely fresh sheets, my eyes rest on the dead African violet on the windowsill and it hits me. I've been going about this superficially. If I'm a dying plant, I've only been considering my leaves—I haven't examined my roots. The truth of the present is often evinced in the seeds of the past. I need to go back to the beginning.

I was born early. I wasn't due until the end of June, but when my mother had her ob-gyn appointment on Friday, June 6, her doctor told her he was going to be out of the country for the following two weeks, so it'd be one of his colleagues who performed the delivery—unless she wanted to be induced. My due date was still a ways away, but it'd be all right if they shaved off some time.

She agreed. There's a picture of her standing with my father in the driveway of our old house on Jason Street later that same afternoon.

They're posed by the car, ready to go, my mother in a tomato-red mini-dress with a round tomato-red suitcase by her feet. She's always had an elegant and playful sense of style. In one of my favorite photographs, she's standing with my dad at Lake Winnipesaukee, wearing a black-and-white polka-dot bikini to match the dalmatian sitting beside them.

She was twenty-six, and this, her first experience with childbirth, was not easy. There were multiple attempts with forceps involved, and my skull has always been mildly misshapen as a result. It was as if the baby inside her was not quite ready to come out.

I've been called a late bloomer, and for a long time—perhaps the first thirty years of my life—I had a deep-seated feeling of being "not ready." So it was amusing to learn that my state of unreadiness extended all the way back to my first moments on earth.

I was an ugly baby. I looked like a cross-eyed troll with male-pattern baldness. Even my mother, who has never been known for sugarcoating her opinions, apologetically admits that I looked "undercooked." It's hard not to feel bad for a first-time mom who was handed a newborn that looked like that. I didn't just have a face like a half-chewed piece of gum; I was also impossible to appease and prone to projectile vomiting. I cried like it was my duty to announce the apocalypse, and anything they put inside me came right back out again. The only varieties of baby food I would eventually allow in my mouth were orange (high in vitamin A)—sweet potato or apricot medley or carrot puree—and even they didn't stay in me for long. Apparently, during a visit to my father's parents in Tampa, I'd thrown up orange on their white carpet so often that by the time we left the whole place looked like a giraffe.

Still staring at the wilted leaves of the African violet, I start to wonder if any of my errors could be inborn. Perhaps I should consider my genes.

I call my mom.

"Girl?" she says, picking up on the first ring. My mother tends to call me one of three things: *Girl*, *Firstborn*, or *Lethal*.

"Hi, Mom." When I ask how she's doing, she tells me that the neighbors have done something new to redirect their rainwater onto her land, and she wants to redo the kitchen, but there are other things she has to do first that are preventing her from beginning, and her heart arrhythmia is somewhat improved but still not great. I cut to the chase.

"Do we have any genetic illnesses in the family?"

"None that I know of—or, if we do, they're well hidden. Why?"

"I know we don't have any obvious ones. But do we know if Nana's father had hereditary hemochromatosis? Before he died in the Spanish flu pandemic?"

"I don't think so. I've never even heard of that."

I mention hemochromatosis—an iron-storage disease—because I've read that it's one of the things that can affect the liver, and I still have a constant ache where my liver should be.

My mother seems defensive about my coming at my illness from a genetic angle. "Does this mean they still haven't figured out what's wrong with you?" she asks, and magically pivots the conversation from questions about our family history to her displeasure with my life choices. If I had a day job, like a normal person, perhaps I would never have gotten sick. My mother also thinks I was a fool to get rid of all my stuff, and I never should have sold my house, which "probably wasn't all that moldy," and, anyway, if I *was* going to sell it, I should have sold it to her. To be honest I don't tend to call my mother that much because I already feel awful, and talking to her can sometimes make me feel worse.

"There's some schizophrenia, on your father's side," I hear her say, no doubt with greater alacrity than if the mental illness were matrilineal.

"You mean that cousin of his—the one who tried to poke her mother's eyes out?"

"Yes."

After we get off the phone, I decide to have my genetic SNPs analyzed by a doctor who's had a lot of success with autistic kids. SNP is shorthand for single nucleotide polymorphism, which is a mouthful way of saying a small genetic defect that can impair your health at the core level—in your cells.

This concept makes all kinds of sense to me. What if I have bad SNPs that have been hobbling me all my life? What if my cells were limping along as best they could for forty years, till they finally hoisted the white flag and cried: *Enough!*

I become convinced that if I just learn which SNPs I have and see which enzymes are underperforming, I can strengthen those enzymes with the appropriate nutrients, and my body will start working again. A month ago, I didn't even know what a SNP was. Now I've learned a whole new language. I'm on the health boards every day, chatting about how I'm heterozygous for both Mthfrs and homozygous for AGT and SLC19A1.

On the boards, I get advice from these incredibly knowledgeable fellow sufferers—people who've dealt with my exact genetic weaknesses and know various things I can take to compensate. Filled with excitement, I call my sisters. Do they want to hear about my SNPs? After all, my genetic weakness could be their genetic weakness, too. I expect this new terrain to be as fascinating to them as it is to me.

But no—my sisters don't want to hear about my SNPs. They're not sick; sickness is a dark continent they not only don't wish to visit, they're not sure they want to read the brochure. Also, two of them have four children each, so they already have more than enough to deal with every day. From where they sit, it seems as if every week, I have a new illness—first it was mold sickness, then parasites, now this. My sisters and I are close in a lot of ways, but my illness has only underscored the separateness of our journeys.

When I leave the bed, I go one of two places: Whole Foods or church. If, on any given day, I can summon the strength to go to *both* Whole Foods *and* church—that is a mighty day indeed. My uniform is black yoga pants and a charcoal cashmere sweater that my ex-boyfriend gave me for Christmas.

The parking lot at Whole Foods is always full, but I know it'd be wrong to take a handicapped spot. While I am, in effect, handicapped, there's always the possibility of becoming worse off. Recently, I read a line in a book that said: "If we all threw our problems in a pile and saw everyone else's, we'd grab ours back."

Midway through the produce jungle, I decide it's time to ramp up my use of food as medicine. Ever since I went to the mold doctor, I've been avoiding simple carbs and gluten. But a diet shouldn't just be about what you take *out*; it should be about what you put *in*. I whip out my new credit card and use it to load up on organic beets, spinach, Swiss chard, carrots, sweet potatoes, mustard greens, almonds, chia seeds, frozen berries, bone broth, rice bran, figs, and tea. I become accustomed to buying foods whose labels repeat the word *free*: gluten-free, grain-free, dairy-free, GMO-free, and soy-free. I find spaghetti made of quinoa, cookies made of almond flour, cereal made of amaranth. Even just standing by my cart in line, I feel virtuous.

At home, I become a veritable juicing machine, determined to conquer whatever's ailing me with superhuman nutrition.

The first thing I notice while on this diet is I can no longer sleep through the night. Also, I have a near-constant need to urinate. I figure this is a side effect from all the juice, plus all the detoxing. There are fierce battles being waged inside me; how could I sleep peacefully when my juiced-up fighter cells are annihilating an enemy?

But before long, I start to feel much, much worse—worse in ways I hadn't even thought possible. If before it felt like I was dying, now it feels like I'm already dead and in hell, where fresh rainbows of pain are dispatched hourly. I feel so bad I actually break down and call my mother. "Mom," I say, my voice barely a whisper, and when she asks what's wrong, I just cry.

We meet for dinner at a restaurant in Arlington Center. We can't meet at her house, because my mom has a difficult time letting go of the past, and when you have a difficult time letting go of the past, clutter happens. And clutter multiplies. By now, it's reached the point where no one is allowed inside her house, not even us kids.

As soon as she sees me, her eyes go wide. "You look terrible. What happened?"

Now that she's in her seventies, she's beginning to have some short-term memory problems. New things, such as my illness, sometimes slip through the sieve of her mind, but her memories of the past are still sharp as knives.

"I'm sick."

"With what?"

"No one knows."

To her credit, she doesn't ask if it's contagious. I would, if I were her. There's nothing like being chronically ill to bring out your inner germophobe.

"Well, you look awful."

"Thanks."

She leans forward, hanging over my side of the table. "Why are you squinting at the menu?" she asks. "Do you need glasses?"

"I don't need glasses; it's the light. The light in here hurts my eyes."

"That's impossible. The light in here is fine."

"It may be fine for you, but it hurts me."

"You're always so dramatic."

I close the menu. "Mom, look at me. I'm sick and I'm scared and I'm in a lot of pain. Could we just—could we please not argue?"

But arguing is what we do best, it seems. It's been this way since I was a teenager. After my mother and father's bitter divorce, there was a ten-year court battle over money. It was my mother versus Goldman Sachs, my mother deposing Bob Rubin. No one thought my mother would win. But she did.

I don't often admit it, but there's a lot of my mother in me. The way she held on during that legal battle—her single-minded determination to keep going and keep fighting until she got what she believed was right. In spite of the odds being stacked against her, in spite of running out of money, in spite of mortgaging her life and living a minimalist existence while the years ticked by and we all grew up and moved away, she won.

When I was little, I found her to be distasteful, like a woman on fire. But now that I've become a woman on fire myself, I realize it's not only tasteful but necessary. A woman on fire is a woman who speaks, who is not cowed, who is not too polite, but who takes the reins of her life into her hands and blazes brightly.

But her victory came at a cost. She has never been able to let go of that battle; it's a pain that never fully leaves. It rooted her, in a sense, in those years. Even now, within hours of meeting someone new, she might feel inclined to whip out letters my father wrote her or other items from her stash of "court-case documents." Although her adversary is long deceased, the fight lives on inside her. I would like her to empathize with what's going on with me. But she's still embroiled in her own battles.

When the waiter arrives, I order a steak. Somehow, with all my juicing and vegetable eating, I seem to have let my meat consumption slip. The steak tastes great—and feels great, too. When I get home, for the first time in a long time, I sleep through the night. In the months that follow, I discover the truth isn't delivered all at once, like a cosmic scoop of mashed potatoes slopped on your plate. More often it arrives piecemeal, bit by bit, one french fry at a time.

My birthday comes and goes, and I still don't know what's causing my symptoms.

"Before you throw in the towel," my friend Amy S. suggests, "why don't you go see a functional-medicine doctor?" When I don't understand the concept of functional medicine, she explains it to me. They look for the root cause of things. When you go to the doctor with a tack in your foot, the mainstream approach is to give you a drug to erase the pain of the tack. The other approach—the one favored by functional medicine—is to find the tack and remove it.

So I go to a functional-medicine doctor in Wellesley, Massachusetts, and he tries to find my tack. And lo and behold, when he shows me my test results, it's a revelation. It turns out that my gut is all out of whack—high yeast, low stomach acid, fermentation, inflammation—in other words, a Disneyland for pathogens.

But that's not all. All the indicators point to one thing: excess oxalates.

"Oxalates?" I say. "What's an oxalate?"

An oxalate is a highly reactive crystal found in many plants that can muck up your metabolism. They're associated with kidney stones, but they actually do all sorts of bad things. As the doctor utters these words, a creeping sensation makes my spine tingle.

"And . . . in what plants are oxalates found, exactly?"

Oh, oxalates are found in lots of things, but they're especially high in beets, spinach, Swiss chard, carrots, sweet potatoes, mustard greens, almonds, chia seeds, berries, rice bran, figs, and tea.

That's right. Almost every single food I've been putting in my mouth is extremely high in oxalates.

"Are you kidding me? But those foods you just named are all the foods I eat! Those foods are all healthy!"

No. Spinach is not healthy. Spinach is practically poison—to me—and so is its evil pal, rhubarb.

I nod, quietly deciding that when I get home, I'll google "my green smoothie is killing me" and decide for myself if this guy is a quack or maybe onto something. Meanwhile, as an experiment, I go back to eating turkey and rice and cheese and cauliflower and pork and chicken and yogurt and ice cream and other very low-oxalate things.

But, regardless of oxalates, something else is amiss, because I was seriously sick well before that bra-strap-showing moldie set me on a path toward mainlining plant toxins.

"Yes," he says, nodding. "Something else *is* amiss." But it's like any good mystery; the resolution doesn't come with the reveal of a single culprit. There are means, motive, and opportunity to explore. The truth doesn't just materialize; this doctor needs time to unravel it.

AN EXPLOSION
OF LIGHTBULB
MOMENTS

After changing my diet, I am clearly on the road to recovery. My pain
levels are cut in half, and I have more energy and am sleeping better
than I have in years. This gives me the strength to explore more possible root problems, and my doctor and I discover I have nearly all the
symptoms of iron overload—anxiety, racing thoughts, loss of appetite,
insomnia, feelings of doom, yeast overgrowth, headaches, aches and
pains, tinnitus. The experience of sharing my symptoms with a physi-
cian who trusts my reportage as much or more than any test result is
both shocking and delightful.

I make an appointment with a nutritionist.

"Your skin has a yellow cast," she says, holding up my forearm.
"Haven't you noticed?"

As a matter of fact, I *have* noticed, both on my own and when
my sister asked: "Have you been using a really bad fake tanner?" But I
figured it must be related to liver failure or something, because, in spite
of all the tests, it has felt so much like my liver's failing.

The nutritionist tells me it's bronzing—another symptom of iron overload. When she tests me for hereditary hemochromatosis—a genetic condition that causes the body to absorb too much iron—I've inherited one of the genes. Hereditary hemochromatosis was on my radar months ago, but when I had blood tests for the iron markers—ferritin, percent saturation, TIBC—that usually tip people off to hemochromatosis, my levels were consistently within range. But my manganese RBC was low. "Maybe it's not the iron per se that matters," I suggest to the nutritionist. "Maybe it's the iron to manganese ratio."

Maybe. Meanwhile, she outlines ways we can bring my iron down and bring up my energy. The metals in your system function like a Jenga tower: slide one out and move it to the top, and you risk toppling the whole thing. High iron leads to high levels of oxidative stress, which can seriously deplete zinc and vitamin B6, which disables various enzymes, and on and on. It turns out to be complicated to sort out my system, and there are many supporting players.

But, for me, the real game changer is vitamin B1. When I take high doses of B1, it's as if I become a new person. The pain, the mental anguish, the crushing fatigue—they literally vanish. I don't just feel better than I did before I got sick; I feel better than I ever have. *Is this the way other people have felt all along?*

I go back to the nutritionist. I'm almost in tears. "I don't understand," I say. "What's happening?"

She explains that we've been adding iron to the food supply in the United States—all grains and pasta are iron "enriched"—since World War II, and some people, like me, have a tendency to absorb it. Meanwhile, the pesticide glyphosate—found in nonorganic food—depletes manganese. Certain supplements can help power up the energy cycle and get the iron moving again.

I'm incredulous. "How can iron overload be behind all these symptoms when no one's even *heard* of it?" I ask.

"Because the solution involves mineral rebalancing, and minerals are unpatentable and cheap." She picks up the bottle of zinc, which costs ten dollars. "There's no money in it for drug companies, so no double-blind studies and no education and no PR."

"This seems like a crime," I say.

"It is."

It's not an instant cure-all. The feeling of magical recovery ebbs and flows, and I know it's something I'll have to work at. But I can tell I'm on the right path. One day, I find myself remembering the prescription vitamins the oncologist gave my dad when he was dying—all the bottles were clearly marked *iron- and copper-free.* Apparently, cancer patients also have trouble metabolizing certain minerals properly.

I go to see another doctor at a treatment center where they specialize in energy rebalancing. I'm still not completely well, but a new hope has infused my cells: *Someone is listening. We're figuring out what's wrong. We're going to fix me.* On the way, I call the Last of the Last Great Men and leave a message. He's gone from my life, but I want him to know what's happening; it feels important. "They figured out what's wrong with me," I say, holding back tears.

THE LONELY GIRL'S GUIDE TO THE COSMOS

When I lost my home and everything I owned, it didn't kill me. They brought a dumpster to my front lawn, and as every book and every photograph and every item of clothing I'd ever owned went into it, I was not sad. All I wanted was to feel okay again, and if feeling okay meant losing everything—if it meant I had to experience a miniature death in order to spring back to life, so be it. *Take it,* I felt my body saying, as my past went into the bin. *Take it all.*

Now, I marvel at how little of that stuff I miss. A whole house's worth—thirty years of possessions. There is one leather belt I occasionally wish I still had because it was uniquely pretty, and, it turns out, uniquely pretty leather belts are hard to come by. But that's about it.

Cash is easier to miss. I've avoided tabulating the precise amount I spent on treatments and supplements because it's too discouraging. I started to add it all up once, but when I got to twenty thousand dollars, I lost momentum and decided to take a bath.

I know I'm not alone. Similar things are happening to countless others. Many people get mold sickness and slowly realize that their mycotoxin-laden belongings are detrimental to their health. Or they get Lyme disease that goes undiagnosed for years. Or they're debilitated by chronic fatigue (myalgic encephalomyelitis), fibromyalgia, multiple chemical sensitivity. The ranks of people like me are, sadly, growing every day.

I've reached the point where I've regained my health—I've been taking my supplements and only using my blender for milkshakes—but I'm still here, by myself, in this generic residential hotel. Without a job and without a real home, I'm aimless. I have more energy, and I can feel the stirrings of a new beginning, but I don't know where to go or what to do.

Then one cold New England afternoon, it hits me. It hits me with the force of something so perfect, so obvious, that at first I'm blind to it—like my own glasses sitting in front of my own face.

I'll take my dog and go to California.

California is appealing for several reasons. The climate's great, all three of my sisters live there now, and it's far away from the familiar things I've known and lost. Maybe going somewhere new will help me start my life over again.

Packing is incredibly easy. I stick the pile of clothes I've bought since leaving the house behind in a paper bag and bring my ExtraBucks coupons to CVS to buy a traveler's toothbrush, a cooler, and an umbrella. I'm not sure why I'll need the umbrella, exactly, since I'll be spending most of my time in a car, but it's on sale and it looks pretty, so I add it to my cart. I also add a two-pack of paper towels, a flashlight, and an iPhone car charger. I would buy some of their beef jerky, but it isn't organic, so I leave it on the shelf with all the other glyphosate-tainted food. When I get home, I fill another paper bag with smaller Ziploc bags that hold my birth certificate, passport, and tax records.

On the day I've chosen to hit the road, my mother calls. I'm at the Honda dealer, getting my CR-V serviced, which was something I figured I should do before driving it three thousand miles. Unfortunately, I only figured this after I'd already loaded it up with my paper bags of worldly possessions, my cooler full of organic apple juice, my comforter, my pillow, my Thieves oil for moldy hotels, my road map, my dog's paraphernalia, and my dog. So now the Honda guys are servicing my loaded-up vehicle while I circle the parking lot with Josie-Jo on her leash. When I see my mother's number on the phone, I'm not sure I should take the call; calls from my mother do not always go well. But I'm in a bold and adventuresome mood, so I do.

"Lethal?" she says.

"Hi, Mom."

"How's the job hunt going?"

"The job hunt's on hold. I've decided to move to California."

"You what? Is this a joke?"

"I want to start over. I need to go somewhere new."

"Don't you think you should get a job before you do anything else?"

"No. See, when you have a job, that's exactly when you *can't* drive cross-country. Why would they want you driving cross-country when they want you slicing pickles or plucking chickens or whatever?"

"You need a job, Girl. Driving cross-country is the last thing you should do. It's irresponsible and immature. I'm surprised you—"

"Gotta go now, Mom. Bye."

She's right. I need a job. I had a job, that wonderful job at the magazine, but it was in publishing, and jobs in publishing have become labors of love where every day you toil beneath the Sword of Damocles. So after thirteen wonderful years, my proofreading job came to an end.

Then I got sick and lost all my money. And now I'm hitting the road and starting life over again.

My mother does not approve of this plan. She has become obsessed with my job status. Part of her preoccupation stems from the fact that I've asked her if I could borrow some money. She said no, because she practices something known as "tough love," which is really just "tough luck," but the people who practice it stick the word "love" on there to make it sound nice. I think it's a little unfair of my mother to keep all her money, especially since most of it was earned by my father, who didn't like her all that much in the end. But, even though I think it's unfair, what other people choose to do with their money is really none of my business.

My mother isn't the only person I've asked to borrow money. When I was sick, I approached a few friends for help getting back on my feet—a gesture my mother refers to as "begging," adding that I should feel ashamed. But I don't feel ashamed; I stopped feeling ashamed when I was sick—that was the gift of my illness. So now, even though I'm poor, I'm rich.

The car is ready. I open my wallet and try to remember which credit card still has a few crumbs left while reassuring the dog over and over that these men are "friends." Josie, my ten-pound hound, thinks it's her duty to bite any man who comes within three feet of me. I've tried to disabuse her of this notion, but she's a dachshund, and they have their own ideas about things.

I turn to one of the mechanics, whose name tag says *Fred*.

"Does this thing have a spare tire?"

"It does." Fred shows me where the secret spare is stashed while giving my dog the side-eye.

"Is she friendly?" he asks.

I can feel the dog's vocal cords rumbling beneath my fingertips.

"Oh, yes," I say. "Very."

I stick the Jink in her crate, buckle myself in, and unfold my map. Then, in a flash, I fold the map back up again. *What was I thinking?* Maps have always confused and depressed me; I have never once had a good experience with a map. I don't know why I even bought a map, when my car has GPS navigation and this isn't the 1980s.

I'm going to do the trip in six legs. At least, that's what I think at the outset. My plan is this:

Boston to Rochester;
Rochester to Toledo, Ohio;
Toledo, Ohio, to Des Moines;
Des Moines to Denver;
Denver to Las Vegas;
Las Vegas to LA.

It's three in the afternoon. A bag of beef jerky sits on the dash. I put the key in the ignition, start the engine, and go.

MEDITATION

The first leg of my journey, Boston to Rochester, is an easy six-hour haul, I-90 all the way. It's relaxing. Driving has always been a contemplative act for me; something about it seems to get the mental gears rolling.

I snap on the radio, curious for news of the world, but all the stations are discussing politics. I listen for a while, but before long it becomes discouraging, and I snap it off. The sky is more interesting. In the distance, banks of white clouds neither approach nor recede but seem to hover motionless as I speed beneath them.

I haven't forgotten all the people on the health boards, all those souls who are still sick. It's as if we were in this unfathomable hell together, and somehow I got out. Sometimes I feel sorry that I'm escaping to my new life and leaving them behind. I want to help them, but I don't know how yet. So for now, I just carry them with me.

The sun melts into the Massachusetts hills. I keep the radio off. I keep on driving.

By hour five, it's clear that this amount of driving is tantamount to a master class in meditation. As the miles glide by, I roll down the windows, letting the warm breeze blow through the car. Then I imagine it blowing through my mind. This feels good, and I think, *Yes—let's wipe the slate clean, do things right this time*. With nothing but open road before me, I attempt to let go of any anger, resentment, or pain; to forgive everyone everything; to love the earth and all it contains. I imagine all the cluttered thought patterns that have been holding me back as strings of empty beer cans dragging behind my car, and, with each mile, more and more of the clattering cans snap off. I'm not sure if this is the proper way to meditate, but it feels right. As the wind whips through the windows, a lifetime of empty beer cans drops away, until my state of consciousness is a radiant white page—no grudges, no enemies, nothing. My hair is flying in all directions, and later, I know it'll take over an hour to get all the tangles out. But my mind is clean.

I'm not sure what I'm supposed to think about, now that I've achieved this pristine state. Frankly, it makes me nervous. What do you feed a virginal brain? I consider trying to recite the Declaration of Independence or looking up the maxims of Immanuel Kant or something.

I'm free to contemplate anything in the multiverse, and after a truck passes me sporting images of the mud-flap girl, I find myself thinking about the pole dancer who shares my name. She was brought to my attention after several people in my life delicately asked if I did a little pole dancing "on the side." The third time this happened, I broke down and entered my own name into the YouTube search field, and, a second later, I was presented with a woman doing this . . . dance. After watching it, I couldn't believe the people who'd asked had been so sheepish. I wanted to go back to them and say: "Are you serious? You thought that was *me*? This is the happiest day of my life." I find it nearly incomprehensible that they believed I was capable of doing those things. I'm not athletic; I'm a person who routinely needs help screwing the plastic caps off drinks. I don't think I could even pole dance in the abstract. Can an object at rest suddenly and spontaneously spiral up a pole? My answer would be no—and the mere fact that I think of pole dancing in physics terms is incriminating. Can a woman perform graceful acts of athleticism while wearing ten-inch heels and an outfit made entirely of plastic? Again, I'd have said no. But I'd have been wrong—so wrong.

I pull off at a Citgo station and tell the dog I'll be right back. Fortunately, the breezy September weather is perfect for briefly leaving a dog in a car. It's good to walk about, to have the blood flow back into my legs. While I use the facilities, I'm feeling mildly successful. So far, driving cross-country is just like everything else in life: When you're outside it, it seems like some big, daunting thing. But once you're inside it, it's nothing.

When I get back to the car, the dog has vomited. "Jinky!" I say, and snuggle her, because she has downcast ears, as if she's done something wrong. In spite of her emotional problems, she's a devoted companion. And she's smart; she knows things. True, she sometimes forgets to put her tongue all the way back in her mouth, so she'll be walking around with her lips closed but her tongue sticking out, which doesn't give the finest impression. But appearances can be deceiving.

I put her in the dog sling that she likes to ride around in—a black canvas sack that resembles a BabyBjörn—and grab my handy roll of paper towels from the back. I try to dampen a paper towel with the bottle of water I just bought, but, as usual, the cap is soldered on, so I have to ask the guy at a nearby pump to twist it off for me. As I approach, holding the Josie-Jink, she growls and bares her teeth at him as if she has rabies, so I smile a lot, and cover her eyes with the palm of my hand, which sometimes helps.

After I clean up the vomit, I take the dog for her walk, which involves multiple sniff stops to investigate unsavory items. It pays to be vigilant while walking the Jink; her idea of a good time is to wolf down a six-month-old hot dog when no one is looking. She seems her usual spunky self, which is a relief. After she does her business, I fill the tank and slide back in the driver's seat. Only thirty miles till Rochester, where

I've booked a pet-friendly motel I found on BringFido.com. The next morning, freshly showered but wearing the same white T-shirt and blue jeans, I'm on the road again.

Day two starts out upbeat. The sun is shining; my gas tank is full. I wish I could drink a huge steaming mug of coffee, but that's forbidden until my adrenals have fully recovered, so I try to imagine myself drinking it, in case there's anything to be gleaned from the placebo effect.

The morning passes uneventfully, and I stop for lunch. I buy a roast beef sandwich at a rest stop in Erie, Pennsylvania, where they sell sandwiches, motor oil, elf statues, bikini calendars, and souvenir mugs that say *PENNSYLVANIA: Once Delaware Dies, We'll Be the Oldest.* The checkout counter is stocked with lottery tickets and tabloid magazines. I'm half tempted to buy a lottery ticket, but I resist. My friend's neighbor in Nahant, Massachusetts—an elderly woman who owned a small convenience store—was recently evicted from her apartment and became homeless after she went bankrupt from scratching all her shop's lotto cards. When I heard her story, I instantly understood the temptation, and was surprised more convenience-store owners didn't fall into the same predicament.

For some reason—could be the clever mugs—this is quite the popular rest stop. There's a line of people ahead of me in baseball caps and flip-flops, waiting to buy their packaged snacks. While I wait, I eye the tabloids, one of which claims that John Travolta is being haunted by the ghost of his long-dead love, Diana Hyland, who died in his arms just as *Saturday Night Fever* was beginning to shoot.

I say a quick prayer for Diana Hyland, and one for John Travolta, too. This is already the longest I've been out of the house in two years.

Back on the road, I'm more than halfway to Toledo. Rochester, New York, to Toledo, Ohio, is another straight shot—sixish hours on I-90 as it follows the southern basin of Lake Erie through Buffalo and

Cleveland. As I merge onto the highway, I notice the bumper sticker on the SUV in front of me: *Honk if you love Jesus. Text and drive if you want to meet him.* I'd like to take a picture of it for my scrapbook, but I'm already juggling my roast beef sandwich, my dog who wants to eat my sandwich, the steering wheel, and a drink. Adding a cell phone to the mix would likely lead to a death-by-phone event that'd be a little too ironic. Fortunately, it feels as if my whole life has been preparing me for this drive. I've done all kinds of things while operating a car, including eating matzo ball soup and changing into a cocktail dress—though not at the same time.

I finish my sandwich, ball up the wrapper, sip my drink till the straw sucks air. I keep on driving.

When I get to Toledo, Ohio, I sleep in a Country Inn & Suites that I again find on BringFido.com, and my dog sleeps in the bed with me. She burrows nose-first under the sheets and curls herself into a crescent moon.

The next day is bright and sunny, but the drive itself is a bit of a blur. In the movies, cross-country driving is exciting and has a soundtrack. In real life, there's a whole lot of road. Toledo, Ohio, to Des Moines, Iowa, is a long haul, longer than I'd expected, and I spend most of it chewing on jerky and trying to come up with a plan for my new life. I need to figure out a way to make money. I have to pay back my friends, while also making rent and buying food.

I could write personalized wedding vows for couples who want something original but don't want to do it themselves. If they liked, I could do it in iambic pentameter, but that'd cost extra.

I could organize people's closets for them. I love to organize things, and am secretly a neat freak. As a no-cost bonus, I'd be willing to go through their cabinets and make sure all the cans have the labels facing out. I've never understood why some people shelve their food with the labels facing every which way. How can they live like that?

I could go to people's homes, sniff their things, and let them know if they have a hidden mold problem. It's a talent I've developed.

As I drive, coming up with incredibly viable life plans, the dust is changing. The dust, the light, the vegetation. The red dirt from the road hovers in my rearview like the ghost of the life I'm leaving behind. The highway isn't all that different from the highways back east. True, all the empty terrain makes it feel as if I've landed in the desert or on the moon, but the ads for Arby's and Taco Bell provide a sense of continuity. The gas station signs are completely different out here, though—way up high, halfway to outer space, probably so travelers can see them from far away, since there can be such long stretches between exits.

I spot a diner by the side of the road and pull off. In general, it's a big waste of time, while traveling cross-country, to actually haul off, sit down, and eat somewhere. But I'm going to live life differently now. I'm not going to wait to enjoy the journey.

I kill the engine, step out of the car, and stretch. Stretching in the sunlight feels cosmically wonderful, and I wonder if it'd be too weird to just drop and do a little yoga right here. It would, but I'd do it anyway, if I wasn't hungry. I amble inside, feeling victorious because I've made myself walk around, if only for a few seconds, before sitting down again.

As soon as I open the menu, which is ten pages long, I'm glad I came. I didn't plan on eating at this particular diner when I set out for California, but every journey has secret destinations of which the traveler is unaware.

The place is steamy and bustling; the air around me hums. I've always felt there was something magical about diners, especially ones like this that have mammoth menus and are open twenty-four hours. *Any kind of food you'd like! Any time, day or night!* If I were the kind of writer who wrote stories where there was a wormhole to another universe, I'd definitely put it in a diner.

My waitress has red hair and is named Frances, which is strange, because, before he met my mother, my father was engaged to a redhead named Frances. Fischer and Frances—only everyone called her Fran. This was back in the days when, at cocktail parties, if they asked my father what he did, he'd say, "I search." When they replied, "You search? Search for what?" he'd say, "For truth."

But Fran died before my father could marry her. One day she had trouble stepping off a curb, and when they went to the doctor, they were told she had ALS—Lou Gehrig's disease. He still had her wedding dress in his closet when my mother first met him. I often think about her, because in a way, like my mother, she also gave me the gift of life. Had she not died, I would never have lived.

This Frances, my waitress, strides forcefully toward me. On the menu, there's something called Millenium Pie, which sounds fantastic—it's made of coconut, pineapples, and custard—but the word *millennium* is misspelled. During my thirteen years as a proofreader, I must have corrected *millennium* a thousand times. Usually I object to eating things that are misspelled, on principle, but I decide to make an exception for Millenium Pie, which, as expected, is delicious.

In the bathroom, the walls are full of graffiti, and there's the inviting presence of a Sharpie dangling from a string. On a spot by the door, I write: *Punishment is a useless weapon in the struggle for people's minds*, just

to mess with people. Decades ago, I wrote that phrase on the wallpaper of my childhood bedroom when I was grounded and angry about it. Writing it again spurs something in me, and, when I get back on the road, suddenly I'm remembering my childhood bedroom, and how we used to sneak downstairs to watch TV when we were kids. I remember all the shows we used to love, how even the commercials were mesmerizing. *I'm a pepper. He's a pepper. She's a pepper. We're a pepper. Wouldn't you like to be a pepper, too?* I remember the mossy, Massachusetts smell in the soil behind my house. I remember the year I painted a triangular rock green, and presented it as a Christmas gift to my third-grade teacher, Mr. Zammarchi, because I secretly loved him. I remember the first sentence I ever wrote in my first journal. *Paul Addezio is the handsomest boy in class.* What caught my eye about Paul was that he arrived on the first day of school with his arm in a cast. I remember my mother's beautiful painting of a young boy that hung in our living room forever, and how surprisingly good it was. I remember the Valentine's Day, before everything fell apart, when she made a mock issue of *Time* magazine with a drawing of my father on the cover under the words *Man of the Year.* I remember my father standing beneath the pale-yellow bulb at the kitchen sink, doing dishes with his back to us while we ran in circles throughout the house. I remember the year we kept the Christmas tree up for so long that first we discussed decorating it with valentines, then shamrocks, then Easter eggs. I remember the Sunday we got all the way home from St. Eulalia's before turning around and driving back because we realized we forgot Paige. I remember watching a bullfight one summer in Spain, and how the death of the bull made me cry. I remember the day I shoplifted a clog (my friend Lisa shoplifted its mate) and then ordered french fries at the restaurant next door with the clog stuffed down my parka, until the Polish shop owner walked in and very politely asked for it back. I remember the blizzard of '78, and how the snow in the yard went all the way up to the top of the fence. I've never seen snow like that, before or since. I remember the billows, the drifts, the thrill of no school for days, the fabulous wonderment of all that snow.

I remember my nana looking at herself in the mirror one day and telling me that when you grow old, on the outside, you look different, but on the inside, you feel exactly the same.

And I remember my dog, my first dog, the one I picked up that day in Pets on Lex when she nuzzled my hair and I just never let her go. On the night I drove her to the vet, that final night, the one when she'd been doing the praying mantis pose, and I knew they were going to put her down, I stroked her fur and whispered in her ear the whole way: "You brought me joy every day" and "I will never love another creature more than I love you."

It's surprising how fresh the memories feel, how close.

After a while, I start to get a little freaked out by all the remembering, because of something my father said shortly before he died: "Your life really does flash before your eyes." I'm worried the memories are some sort of precursor to a car accident, so I try to think about something else, something that isn't a memory, but it's hard, because time is slippery, and sometimes, when I'm in motion like this, it feels as if everything is a memory.

At midnight, I'm still so deep in reverie that I miss the exit for Des Moines and have to circle back around. It's Friday night, and I quickly discover that Des Moines is a college town—the streets are full of students in varying degrees of inebriation. I can tell they're inebriated students because they're wearing neon sticks on their heads and carrying red plastic cups. A line of them links arms in the middle of the sidewalk and shouts up at the crosslight in unison. From my hotel room, I can still hear them hollering down in the street when I pull the blinds shut and turn out the light.

The next day, I don't feel well. My hips are sore, my shoulders tight. I try to jam Josie's stuffed iguana behind my back for lumbar support, but it doesn't work. Also, my feet are becoming a problem. When I was a kid, I named them Karen and Diane, and, by God, once again it's Diane who has to do all the driving.

At eleven in the evening, I'm still more than three hours outside Denver when all of a sudden the beams of oncoming traffic are in my lane. My mind jolts awake, and I grip the wheel, instinctively wanting to swerve but knowing I can't because I'm surrounded by cars. I also know I can't squeeze my eyes shut, so I have to brace for the crash with my eyes wide open. Then, with my body taut, when I don't crash, when I realize that the beams of oncoming traffic are *not* in my lane, but I'm just so tired that I'm starting to have minor hallucinations, I know it's time to get off the road. I take the next exit, which is for North Platte, Nebraska, and pull into the parking lot of a Holiday Inn.

My eyes have grown accustomed to the dark, so the lobby burns with the light of a thousand suns. When I ask about a room, the overnight clerk flatly informs me that there are no more dog-friendly rooms available.

"Are you sure?"

She's sure.

I'm tempted to tell her I don't really have a dog, I was just asking for a friend. But for some reason, I brought Josie in with me, and her little brown face is peering out of her sling.

"But you're the only dog-friendly hotel for miles," I say.

"Sorry," says the clerk. She doesn't even shrug.

"Look at this animal." I step back and lift my hands. "She fits in my purse! She's not really a dog—she's more like a good-natured cat."

"We don't allow cats, either."

"What if I pay for them to clean the room?"

"Sorry. It's policy. I can't break the rules."

This kind of rigid rule-following is not at all my style, but I understand that it's the style of many members of my society.

"Fine," I say, and walk away.

It's approaching midnight. My legs wobble like cooked spaghetti. Karen and Diane are both pissed. Above the parking lot, the skull of the moon lurks behind the cut-the-crap stars. I move the car to a corner of the lot and park beneath the glow of a street lamp, to discourage any would-be killers. It's weirdly hot in North Platte, Nebraska, and the CR-V desperately needs air, but when I crack the windows, the mosquitoes get in, and I don't like this. Being bitten by a mosquito is like sharing a needle with the world.

I recline the seat all the way and prop my pillow in a variety of positions, but the car is so uncomfortable and I'm so annoyed by the clerk's rule-following dogma that I can't sleep. *Couldn't she have just made an exception? Why are human beings such robots?*

Lying sideways in the driver's seat, with my dog mushed between my knees and my face mashed against the door handle, I vow that whenever I'm given a choice between obedience and kindness, I'll choose kindness.

WHEN YOUR
STRUGGLE BECOMES
YOUR SONG

I don't recall Jack Kerouac ever addressing the issue of personal hygiene in *On the Road*. And yet, on any lengthy journey, there are times when the issue of personal hygiene does come up. For instance, on Sunday morning, when I wake bathed in sweat in a steaming-hot car in the parking lot of the North Platte Holiday Inn—a car in which my dog has recently vomited.

I try to clean up the vomit, but I mostly just spread it around. My armpits stink like six-month-old hot dogs. My vehicle doesn't have blackout shades, so to get out of my sweat-drenched clothes, I have to duck and strip while hoping no humans are hiding in the bushes. I give myself a paper-towel-and-shampoo "bath," which involves bracing my feet against the steering wheel and contorting into the kinds of naked positions I'm certain are illegal in some states. Halfway through, I look up and pray to God that that thing on the street lamp above me isn't a mounted camera. Once I'm clean—ish—I reach in the back, pull some black yoga shorts and a yellow tank top out of a paper bag, and slither into them. I dump some bottled water on my toothbrush, run it over my teeth, and spit on the pavement. Deodorant, lip gloss, hair in a ponytail—that'll have to do.

I pull out my phone and enter my zip code into masstimes.org to find the Catholic church nearest me. It is Sunday morning, after all. The St. Patrick's Church of North Platte is only 2.4 miles away. Mass is starting in five minutes.

When I get there, it's too hot to leave the dog in the car, so I bring her in with me, nestled in her sack. When I bless myself with holy water, I splatter some on her snout, hoping this will discourage her from throwing one of her maniacal barking fits in the Lord's house.

The holy water works. For the entire Mass, in a church packed with strangers, including some who are within three feet of me, she sleeps in her sack with only her tail sticking out. No one seems to mind that I've brought a dog in to church with me, or maybe they all just assume I have a demon baby with a hairy brown tail.

I'm underslept and still kind of grumpish, so before they get to the Gospel reading, I try to shift my headspace so I'll be in the right mindset to receive God's word. The gist of today's Gospel is this: Jesus says something that's *pretty* clear but maybe also *sort of* mysterious, and none of the apostles gets it because they're all a bunch of boneheads. Because they're us. We're the apostles.

After Mass, as I emerge into the sunshine, I realize something. I'm not in pain. The light isn't blinding. The celestial loneliness is gone.

I've been lowering my iron burden, and it's working. I whisper a word of thanks that has more presence than anything I said in church. Just feeling okay feels like a miracle.

It's noon. From the parking lot of the St. Patrick's Church of North Platte, Nebraska, to California is a little over a thousand miles. I plan to do half today and the other half tomorrow. Today I'll leave Nebraska, cross Colorado, and enter Utah. Tomorrow I'll cross Utah, zip over the southern tip of Nevada, and enter California. When I get to California, I have only a vague outline of a plan. I'm going to rent an apartment in the town that's mentioned in *Bill and Ted's Excellent Adventure*. I chose it via a mix of inspiration, research, and gut feeling, and I hope that if I can just prove my mettle by making it to the Golden State, the rest of my dharma will reveal itself.

Arriving in California with no possessions, no money, and no boyfriend is not the life I had planned. This is plan B. But life is never the way we dream it will be, the way it looks in movies. It's always wilder and messier and more tangled and confusing and painful and broken and better.

I get the idea that it'd be fitting to listen to some John Denver before I leave Colorado, but Siri misunderstands me and offers up Kenny Rogers instead. That's all right. I can do Kenny. I used to listen to Kenny all the time when I was a kid.

My father's taste in music was so exquisitely unhip that it might actually have come around to being hip again. When I was little, we used to listen to Kenny Rogers, Dolly Parton, Roger Whittaker, and Engelbert Humperdinck. After my father died, I was given a small box of his belongings, and my favorite item, by far, is an old store-bought cassette called *More Christmas Disco*. The mere fact that there existed a compilation of Christmas disco, and that my father had owned it, would have been enough. But he wanted *More*.

The saddest thing about losing him when I was so young is that, when he died, I was not yet fully formed. There are a thousand things I never had the chance to discuss with him, a million conversations. He's been dead for over twenty years now, and when I'm in the stationery aisle and I see cards addressed *To the Greatest Dad on Earth*, I still pick them up and read them.

He never had the chance to read my work. There was only one draft of a story he read—the first story I ever wrote, about me and my sisters. When I gave it to him, he'd been teaching me proofreading marks— which was prophetic—and he used my story as an opportunity to quiz me on what I'd learned. I knew what all the mysterious hieroglyphics meant—the slashes and pointy hats and loop-de-loops—but I was stopped by three open circles in the left-hand margin at the end. I didn't know what three open circles meant. When I asked him, I could tell he'd been waiting to fill me in. "That's where the tears landed," he said.

It's as I'm grooving along to Kenny and reminiscing about my dad that I realize I'm almost out of gas. Heart thumping, I glance around. I'm in Utah. The terrain is super lunar. When I switch to the radio, the dial just spins. My tank is near *E*, and I am, literally, in the middle of nowhere.

I have this way of praying that's not really praying so much as feeling panic and thinking about God. I figure God knows my predicament, since he knows everything, so there's no real need to ask for help *per se*; I just have to turn my attention toward him. I remember almost nothing about *On the Road*, which I read many moons ago, but there is one thing Jack Kerouac said that I'll never forget: "Accept loss forever. Be submissive to everything, open, listening."

I accept. I submit. I listen.

The needle keeps moving in the wrong direction.

And then, just like that, I spot a rest area, way off in the distance. I take the exit and pull up, laughing, both because I'm happy and because the place truly is like a scene from an Old West movie. There's even a sign someone has cleverly designed so it reads *You Are Nowhere* or *You Are Now Here*, depending on how you look.

I walk up to the cash register and plunk down my credit card.

"Pump number three, please," I say.

The one-armed man behind the register pushes my card back.

"Don't take this card here, ma'am."

"What? Why? That's a major credit card."

"Don't take it," he sniffs.

I search my wallet. I have four other credit cards, but none of them has any credit left.

"I'm driving cross-country," I say. "That card has worked everywhere else. Please. It's the only card I have."

The man's mouth has a collapsed look that I realize is from a lack of teeth. "Can't run it, ma'am. Won't nothing work. Maybe it'll work somewhere else."

"Is there another rest stop nearby?"

"Few miles down the highway," he says, looking away.

I stand there, stalling, waiting for the man to look back so I can plead with him with my eyes, because my intuition is telling me not to leave, not to take no for an answer, that this rest area is my only hope. But the one-armed man is waiting for me to get a move on. As I walk away, I catch a tabloid headline declaring that Jennifer Aniston is pregnant and John Cusack has six weeks to live.

I get back on the road with a wary feeling in the pit of my gut that deepens the farther into the desert I go. There's still no cell signal, no sign of any rest stops. The radio dial keeps spinning—I just leave it on and let it spin. As if I needed it, the gas tank "idiot light" has blinked on. I'm beginning to feel an urgent pressure in my intestines. It could be stress, or a delayed reaction to the fish tacos I had for lunch. Not everyone would think it wise to order fish at a tiny Mexican shack in the middle of Nebraska. But I'm special like that.

There's a sign coming up, and I read the little white words as they fly by: *Next rest area 96 miles.*

Wait. That can't be right. The one-armed man said "just down the road." The sign passed so quickly, though—I could have misread it. Maybe the nine was a zero—*06 miles*. It'd be weird to put a zero in front of the number like that, I admit, and that's definitely not the way they do things where I'm from. But maybe they do things differently out here.

My intestines are spasming. Both hands clutch the wheel. I have a dizzying premonition that the next rest area is indeed ninety-six miles away.

Just then the dial, which has been spinning for miles, stops. I'm in shock. There, in the middle of the desert, out of the clear blue sky, I hear the voice of Abba.

That's right—ABBA. And my speakers are both exhorting me to follow the advice of the song "Take a Chance on Me."

It's impossible. Out of all the static in the universe, in my moment of greatest need, *this* is what my receiver pulls down? This was my favorite song when I was seven years old, and I love it even more now. Without thinking, suddenly my mouth falls open, and I'm singing—singing in the face of all the pain and fear and loneliness—singing with all I am, and all I hope to be.

I turn the volume up as high as it'll go, until my car is vibrating as it bounds through the dusty hills of Utah, and I'm not surprised to feel my body filling up with joy, because I know I've entered one of those moments when my struggle becomes my song, and, when that happens, nothing else matters, and no one can touch me. I might even make it to the next rest area, and they might accept my last remaining credit card. Who knows—anything is possible. There are so many times in life when everything goes wrong at once. Maybe there can also be a time when everything goes right.

And in this moment, I realize something. Of course this illness and its legacy will be the invisible journey that in some ways defines me, the pain that never fully leaves. As much as anything, it's our sufferings that shape us and make us who we are. But I have metabolized it into myself now, integrated it. My suffering has become something else—a kind of strength.

I flatten my palm against the glass sunroof, and then, in a flash, my bug-splattered white CR-V becomes a rolling cenacle of prayer. In the middle of the Utah wilderness, at eighty miles an hour, suddenly I'm lifting up my father and Frances and all the sick people on the Internet, and the one-armed man and John Cusack and the Last of the Last Great Men, and then everyone on these roads and everyone alive and everyone who has ever lived. The sun's so bright it's as if the particles of light are breaking through the windshield and into my plasma, until the blue in me merges with the blue in the sky and the faraway sea, and I'm weight-less and free, I'm not even sure I need to go to California anymore, maybe I'll stay like this forever, maybe I'll just keep on driving.

ACKNOWLEDGMENTS

Thanking people at the end of a memoir is strange, because, in a way, you want to thank everyone you've ever known. I got in trouble after my last book for absentmindedly leaving someone out—which I still feel bad about—so allow me to simply say this: if you have been present in my life, thank you. I've finally reached that place of integration where it feels as if everyone I've interacted with has helped me in some way. If you shared your umbrella with me when you saw me standing in the rain on the steps of the Fogg, or gave me a sympathetic smile when I was riding the elevator at Sloan Kettering, or offered me a quarter when I was having a pay-phone meltdown back in 1996, you helped me write this book. Above all, lately I feel an odd, nostalgic affection for the kindred souls who share my vintage: the others who were born in or around 1969. I can feel, now more than ever, that we're all riding the same beam of light.

Special thanks to Lisa Bankoff, who believed in this book from day one and never stopped believing; Jeff Jackson, Michael Voll, and Eric Vrooman, my trusted readers, who have improved everything I've ever written; Mac and Leslie McQuown, whose generosity enabled me to keep writing; Danielle and Helen DeVine, whose prayers have kept me alive lo these many years; and Laura Van der Veer, who not only sought this book out, and knew how to improve it, but toiled to shape it into the thing it always wanted to be—something even I couldn't see. Her fingerprints are on every page. Truly, this is a book with two mothers.

And to Ralph, who was there for me when I needed it most.

ABOUT THE AUTHOR

Photo © Stephanie Girard

Alethea Black was born in Boston and graduated from Harvard College in 1991. Her work has been featured in the *Kenyon Review*, the *American Literary Review*, and *Narrative Magazine*, among others. The author of the short-story collection *I Knew You'd Be Lovely*, she's the recipient of the Arts & Letters Prize and is a three-time winner of the MOTH StorySLAM. Black lives in Los Angeles County, California, with her dachshund, Josie. For more on her work, visit www.aletheablack.com.